THE POLITICS
OF
PRESIDENTIAL APPOINTMENT

ALSO BY SHELDON HACKNEY

POPULISM TO PROGRESSIVISM IN ALABAMA

POPULISM: THE CRITICAL ISSUES

THE POLITICS

OF

PRESIDENTIAL APPOINTMENT

A Memoir of the Culture War

SHELDON HACKNEY

WITH A FOREWORD BY

VERNON E. JORDAN, JR.

NewSouth Books

Montgomery

NewSouth Books
P.O. Box 1588
Montgomery, AL 36102

Copyright © 2002 by Sheldon Hackney
All rights reserved under International and Pan-American Copyright
Conventions. Published in the United States by NewSouth Books, a
division of NewSouth, Inc., Montgomery, Alabama.

Library of Congress Cataloging-in-Publication Data

ISBN 1-58838-068-8

Design by Randall Williams
Printed in the United States of America

TO

LINDA HYATT AND MELANNE VERVEER

WITHOUT WHOSE DEDICATED EFFORTS

THERE WOULD HAVE BEEN NO HAPPY ENDING

Contents

FOREWORD

VERNON E. JORDAN, JR.

IT IS IMPOSSIBLE to turn the pages of this small but important book without being struck by ironies and lessons from the Culture Wars. One of the most interesting to me, a sobering cultural lesson, concerns the campus event that lies at the heart of this book, the infamous "water buffalo" incident. Here is the lesson: the participant in the white mob became a hero for the right wing, while the four black women remained faceless and the objects of national ridicule.

Thankfully, another lesson that emerges from Sheldon Hackney's story is that justice can triumph if people of good will, from the broad center of the political spectrum, have the courage of their convictions and refuse to be intimidated.

I have more than a passing interest in the story you are about to read. Like its author, I am a native Southerner who grew up with an intense interest in history and politics and with a strong desire to bring my native region fully into the Union, to have it embrace not just the rhetoric but the reality of democracy. Unlike its author, I am not white and I did not grow up in his world of middle-class privilege. Nonetheless, the social revolution that changed our country beginning in the 1940s and those mutual interests in history and activism eventually brought the two of us together. Sheldon and I shared a Southern heritage, though we had experienced it from very different perspectives. More importantly, we shared a sense of history and a deep commitment to racial equality. We were interested in not just what America had been, but what it could be.

Sheldon Hackney is a brilliant scholar and an outstanding educator. He had served ably as the president of Tulane University and was in his first year as the president of the University of Pennsylvania when my daughter, Vickee, graduated from the school in 1981. I was the commencement speaker at the graduation ceremonies.

I had also known Sheldon's mother-in-law, Virginia Foster Durr, because of her involvement in the Civil Rights Movement in her hometown of Montgomery, Alabama, and with the Southern Regional Council in Atlanta, Georgia.

Mrs. Durr was a Southern white woman in a class of her own. Her world was that of the old Southern aristocracy, mostly mythic but not altogether. She married Clifford Durr, of a prominent Alabama family, a Rhodes scholar and a lawyer who went to Washington to help FDR bring the nation out of the Great Depression. Mrs. Durr's sister was married to another Alabama lawyer, Hugo Black. In Washington, Mrs. Durr was a close personal friend of Eleanor Roosevelt. The family was well-connected.

However, the Durrs turned their backs on Washington power and prestige during the McCarthy era. Who could ever forget the scene of Mrs. Durr on the witness stand during the Eastland Hearings witchhunt, calmly powdering her nose while ignoring the inquisitors. And then her husband, by then a member of the Federal Communications Commission, displayed his own courage when he was confronted with the regrettable Truman loyalty oath. Durr correctly declared the oath unconstitutional, refused to sign it, and in protest declined President Truman's offer of reappointment.

The Durrs then returned to Alabama just in time to befriend Rosa Parks and to become among the few white Southerners to support the Civil Rights Movement that emerged from the

Montgomery Bus Boycott. In the process, of course, they were ostracized from white society and Durr lost most of his law practice.

I learned most of this history in the mid-1970s, when Mrs. Durr began spending summers with her daughter and son-in-law, Lucy and Sheldon, on Martha's Vineyard. During family vacations there I took great pleasure in revisiting the Civil Rights Movement on a shaded porch with Mrs. Durr and in getting to know the Hackney family. I came to admire and respect Sheldon not only for his humanity but also for his intellect and proven abilities.

In 1992, another of my friends, Bill Clinton, was elected president and he chose me to head his transition team. And that is how I, a black man from humble beginnings in Atlanta, Georgia, became one of the political mentors of Sheldon Hackney, a white man from a more privileged background in Birmingham, Alabama. When Sheldon told me that he was interested in a place in the Clinton administration, I was eager to help him. He was exactly the sort of person who needs to be in the public service: smart, knowledgeable, a proven administrator, thoroughly grounded in the broad center of politics, and an intellectual who could communicate across the spectrum of educational levels and interests.

He was an ideal candidate to head the National Endowment for the Humanities, and I and others on the transition team knew from the start that we had the right person for the job. Of course, we did not anticipate the extent to which he would become a lightning rod for right-wing attacks.

The story Sheldon relates in the pages to come intersects with all the avenues of history, politics, and society that came into sharp focus in what were termed the Culture Wars. And at the outset of the Clinton administration, the Culture Wars were at their most intense.

We should understand the attack on Sheldon not only as part of that ongoing battle but as an attempt to undermine the Clinton presidency. It was not the only such attempt, and not the most important, but it shows in a clear way the machinery of "slander by slogan" at work.

The intense partisanship of some political actors, and the fascination of the press with "controversy," made it impossible for the public to understand the difficult "gray area" issue of how universities must protect the speech rights of less powerful students against the abusive speech of more powerful students.

The partisanship and the controversy combined to make Sheldon's confirmation process one of the most brutal I've witnessed in my thirty years on the national scene.

It is nice that the tortured story you are about to read had a happy ending.

I am proud that Sheldon Hackney was confirmed as chairman of the NEH, and that he served with distinction, vision, and committed leadership. Of course, that came as no surprise to me.

VERNON E. JORDAN, JR., *is senior managing director of Lazard Frere and the author of* Vernon Can Read.

THE POLITICS
OF
PRESIDENTIAL APPOINTMENT

INTRODUCTION

W E ROUNDED THE corner of the broad corridor in the Dirksen Senate Office Building on June 25, 1993, approaching room 430 where my confirmation hearing was to be held. Suddenly we were aware of a crowd and the loud buzz of conversation. People were standing two abreast in a long line stretching almost the length of that mammoth hallway. Martha Chowning, who had worked as an "advance person" in the Clinton campaign and was now the liaison to the White House for the National Endowment for the Humanities, had met me as my taxi pulled up outside, and she was trying to prepare me for the scene I was about to encounter. The hearing room was already jammed with people, she said, and the news media were there in force.

My anxiety level, already high, began to soar. Martha added that some of the crowd had just come from a hostile press conference staged by my opposition in a nearby room provided through the good offices of Senator Trent Lott. Presiding at that counter-hearing were Ralph Reed of the Christian Coalition, who had dubbed me "The Pope of Political Correctness," and Floyd Brown of the Family Research Council, the creator of the infamous Willie Horton advertisement for George Bush's 1988 presidential campaign.[1] Fresh from a successful "Borking"[2] of my friend, Lani

Guinier, the University of Pennsylvania Professor of Law whose nomination to be Assistant Attorney General for Civil Rights they had forced President Clinton to withdraw, they were determined to make my confirmation another major battle in the "Culture War." Though I was a reluctant combatant in the Culture War, I was by then the most visible gargoyle decorating the battlements of the Ivory Tower.

By then I had been mocked on national radio by Rush Limbaugh, denounced in hundreds of newspapers and *Newsweek* by syndicated columnist George Will, excoriated in the *Washington Post* by Charles Krauthammer, flayed alive for television by Pat Buchanan on "Firing Line," and otherwise held up for scorn and derision. The *Wall Street Journal* editorial page, the house organ of movement conservatives, had written seven—count 'em, seven!—unflattering editorials about me and the University of Pennsylvania over the span of a few weeks in April, May, and June, while I stood blindfolded and lashed to the stake. John Leo of *U.S. News and World Report* created a "Sheldon Award," which he annually bestows on the college president who most closely appoximates my profile in cowardice. Whoever formulated the precept that there is no such thing as bad publicity, as long as they spell your name right, could not have had this in mind. I know there are people who think it is worse to be ignored than to be criticized, but I am not among them.

As I walked down the corridor toward my appointment with the Senate Committee, I thought of the Tony Auth cartoon that had appeared in the *Philadelphia Inquirer* just two weeks before. It showed a pride of lions feasting on a carcass labeled "Lani Guinier." Parachuting into the midst of this feeding frenzy was a figure labeled "Hackney." He had a quizzical look on his face as he gazed down at his carnivorous landing zone. I knew exactly how he felt.

Thinking back on that spring-from-hell, I recall it not only as the worst time of my life, but as an out-of-body experience. I followed the story in the press of some idiot named Hackney, who was either a left-wing tyrant or a namby-pamby liberal with a noodle for a spine. My critics couldn't decide which. Not only did I not recognize him, I didn't much like him either. I remember laughing at the headline of a story in the *New York Post* that trumpeted, "Loony Lani and Crackpot Prez." I did not think that Lani was loony, of course, but it was even harder for me to realize that I was the crackpot prez. How could a mild-mannered, unassuming Ivy League president get into such a mess? Even more interesting, how could he get out of the mess?

The story that follows answers those questions. It is an odyssey of sorts, an account of my journey, both geographical and intellectual, from Philadelphia to Washington. It did not take nine years, nor am I the man of many wiles, but there were adventures along that metaphorical I-95, and I will insinuate into the story some of the wisdom gleaned from my encounters.

Though this is a story about a Presidential appointment and Senate confirmation, it cannot be fully understood unless the reader knows something about me and about the university world. Thus, having begun the book with my confirmation hearing, I then backtrack to provide necessary context before returning to the actual confirmation. My primary purpose is to tell my own story in my own way, getting the white hats and black hats on the right heads. I believe my story about an allegedly grotesque example of "political correctness" illustrates how the Culture War and the current media environment combine to polarize public discussion. In that polarized atmosphere, the public has no chance to understand complex issues. Not only are moderates trampled underfoot, but the great gray areas where life is actually lived, the areas of ambiguity and tradeoffs between competing values, are rendered toxic to human habitation. This is not healthy for a democracy.

The only way I have been able to make sense of this brief slice of my life is to think of it as a case study in how the politics of public perception work. Both Left and Right struggle to frame issues advantageously by aligning those issues with prevailing cultural values in a way that will favor their own side. This has always been the case. To the Federalists, the Alien and Sedition Acts of 1798 were about patriotism; to the Republicans, they were about free speech. To the abolitionists, the Civil War was about slavery; to the white South (at least in retrospect), it was about states' rights.

The question is, "How close to the truth should a polemicist stick, and who is to protect the public from unethical distortions?" I will demonstrate how the version of my story that the public heard was created for ideological purposes and then governed as much by the internal dynamics of the media's storytelling, and the intensely bitter partisan atmosphere of 1993, as by any "truth" residing in the events themselves or in the characters featured in the drama.

My tale is set precisely in the era of politics by professional character assassination exposed by David Brock in his recent confessional, *Blinded By The Right: The Conscience of an Ex-Conservative.* Indeed, one might think of my experience as a squirrel hunt in an obscure corner of the forest where the big game hunt was also in progress. The hunting parties overlapped, and the fates of the quarries were linked, but I am not suggesting that the two adventures were of similar significance.

Like most tales told by the protagonist, this is about good versus evil. I naturally hope the reader will cheer for the right side. In a truer sense, however, this is not about an apocalypse, in which the forces of light are arrayed against the forces of darkness. On the contrary, this is a story about the gray area, about how hard it is to be a centrist when the forces of polarization are so strong. It takes place in 1992-1993 when the Culture War was at its most intense.

The reasons for the Culture War itself are not mysterious. First and foremost, it is a counterrevolution seeking to bridge the cultural chasm of the 1960s, the fissure that separates post-Sixties

America from the 1950s. That long decade, from the *Brown* decision in 1954 to the resignation of Richard Nixon as President in 1974, was a flamboyant mixture of nobility and self-indulgence. The Civil Rights Movement and the other social justice movements transformed the monochromatic mainstream into cultural technicolor; but the Civil Rights Movement eventually was shattered by the excesses of black nationalism; the New Left dissolved amidst delusions of revolutionary violence; the anti-war movement, while morally correct, also unsettled America's view of itself as indomitable and righteous. Furthermore, the counterculture created its own opposition by identifying the culture itself as the threat to human freedom, imagining the enemy to be all the verities of middle-class life: the sanctity of the nuclear family, chastity, sobriety, cleanliness, respect for authority, postponed gratification, hard work, and responsibility toward others. Not only have we not yet fully integrated the results of the 1960s into our habits of thought and our daily lives, we are still sorting through the rubble of that decade and arguing about which bricks we want to use to build our new house. Politics in the 1990s were about the attempted transvaluation of America in the 1960s by the forces of change.

Politics, of course, are still about tax codes, the regulation of commerce, and how many public dollars are going to be spent for what purposes in whose district. Aside from domestic security against terrorism, which is not a partisan matter, there are still large and real issues that claim our attention: health care, campaign finance reform, restructuring social security, protecting the environment, and the wisdom and social justice of tax cuts. Still, to an unusual degree, the public arena in the 1980s and 1990s was full of arguments about such things as the Mapplethorpe photographic exhibit that was canceled at the Corcoran Gallery in 1989, the Enola Gay exhibit that was recast at the Smithsonian in 1995, the proposed national history standards that were ambushed in 1996-

97, the "Sensation" exhibit of contemporary British art at the Brooklyn Museum of Art in 1999, the Confederate flag flying over the state capitol in South Carolina in 2000, and such continuing controversies as school prayer, abortion rights, school vouchers, gays in the military, and hate-crime laws. In short, values-in-conflict have been competing with the politics of resource allocation.

One of the ironies of the rise of the New Republicans is that the Cultural Right has successfully copied tactics employed in the 1960s and 1970s by the Cultural Left. The culture, of course, is constantly in motion, pushed and pulled this way and that by innumerable influences, some of them large and impersonal, such as changing technology, but some of them quite self-conscious. For example, the extraordinarily successful women's movement, since its rebirth with Betty Friedan's *The Feminine Mystique* in 1963, proceeded along two fronts at once.[3] One front was public policy. It advocated new laws that were designed to prevent discrimination against women in hiring and in pay, and that were intended to protect women from harassment in the workplace. The notion was that laws would change behavior and behavior would change the culture, an approach pioneered by the Civil Rights Movement.

At the same time, however, the movement assaulted patriarchal biases in the culture directly by attacking the language in which those biases were encoded, and by confronting the manners that were the reflection of the cultural biases. It may have seemed silly to have to use gender-equal "him/her" rather than the privileged "him," and it was a nuisance to learn to use the neutral salutation "Ms." in order to avoid the culturally loaded "Miss" or "Mrs.," but those tactics had the desired consciousness-raising effects. Behaving as if "the personal is political" struck many as bad manners, but it worked. The culture changed in the intended direction. That is why conservatives have anathematized as "politically correct" such linguistic subversion of the existing order.

The Religious Right is following a course similar to the women's movement by seeking to capture the government for some of its purposes (prevention of abortion; teaching creationism in school; protecting prayer in schools; character education), and by waging at the same time cultural warfare in the non-governmental public square over powerful symbols (prayer at public events; the invocation of religiously derived values in public policy debates; respect for the flag; recitation of the pledge of allegiance).

The counterculture of the 1960s, on the other hand, did not trust the government, and disdained the political movements of the Left in the 1960s as well. It simply ran a large-scale cultural demonstration project by turning almost every middle-class virtue upside down, and then singing and living the new lifestyle. "Let your culture be your politics," it said, and bombarded the public with a long string of slogans: "do your own thing"; "if it feels good, do it"; "never trust anyone over thirty"; "tune in, turn on, and drop out"; "make love, not war."

We should not be surprised, therefore, when the counterrevolutionaries of the current Culture War focus upon universities, dedicated as those cultural warriors are to rolling back the cultural changes initiated in the 1960s by feminism, the Civil Rights Movement, the other social justice movements, the anti-war movement, and the counterculture. The revolutionary army seemed to be bivouacked on college campuses in those turbulent years, and universities today are suspected of harboring sixties fugitives who fled the scene of the accident.

Against its will, then, the university is an actor in the Culture War. I use the term "actor" deliberately, because the Culture War is a kind of theater, a theater in which the players plot scenes and follow scripts designed to send cultural messages to various audiences. Just as we spoke of the European Theater and the Pacific Theater in World War II, we now have the *campus theater* in the Culture War. The objective is to pull the culture to the Left or to the Right. The tactic pursued relentlessly by the cultural warriors of the Right is to demonize universities as the breeding ground of the evil forces of liberalism that are undermining "American civilization."

The Culture War is a contest for the minds and hearts of the public. Consequently, it must be waged through the communications media. It is no secret that journalism has been changing, that the proliferation of modes of communication has driven journalists to ever more inventive ways of capturing the public's attention. Entertainment values intrude on the news, sound bites muscle aside thoughtful commentary, and ever shorter news cycles cause a rush to publication without verification. One of the major themes of my story is the difficulty of dealing with complex issues in a media environment that rewards simplicity, one in which the desire for good copy overwhelms the dictates of good sense.

Like all other liberals, I believe that a free press is the bulwark of liberty and democracy. Like anyone who has ever been covered by the press, I am painfully aware that journalists are fallible. Too frequently, reporters don't get the context right, and commentators don't get the facts right. Journalists, I fear, are just as subject as other humans to incompetence, venality and self-deception. It is frequently difficult to know which of those failings is the culprit when a story goes awry.

Those intimations of mortality, however, do not worry me very much; they do not threaten the republic. I am more concerned about a different and more subtle phenomenon in the media world. Here is a simple illustration. In the winter of 1994, after I had been at the National Endowment for the Humanities for about six months, the NEH announced that the Jefferson Lecturer for that spring would be Gwendolyn Brooks, the Chicago poet who, in 1950, became the first African American woman to win the Pulitzer Prize. The Jefferson Lectureship carries a $10,000 stipend and is the most significant award that an American humanist can win. The roster of Jefferson Lecturers is a Who's Who of humane letters. *The New Republic*, edited then by the right-leaning controversialist, Andrew Sullivan, had opposed my nomination. It greeted the news that Brooks would be the Jefferson Lecturer with a full column of sarcasm and ridicule. Charging that Gwendolyn Brooks was not good enough for the honor and that she had been selected only because she is black, *TNR* screamed that this is just what could be expected from a chairman of the NEH who is as hopelessly politically correct as Hackney!

Aside from *TNR's* judgment about a significant American poet and a wonderfully gracious woman, there were two things wrong with this editorial opinion. The Jefferson Lectureship is awarded after careful screening by a committee of the National Council on the Humanities, followed by a discussion and a vote by the full Council. Choosing the Jefferson Lecturer is a privilege that the Council guards jealously. The chairman may participate but cannot control. Second, and more damning, the selection of Ms. Brooks was made several months before I was confirmed, and was made by the thoroughly conservative National Council that had been assembled by Lynne Cheney, my pugnaciously conservative predecessor at the NEH. I had absolutely nothing to do with it.

It is easy to see how *TNR* could make the mistake it made. That Ms. Brooks was my choice fit so well into the story they had been telling about me that they did not bother to check the facts. Truth was the victim of the needs of their narrative. This is the heart of the matter. Something is wrong when the story generates its own facts, rather than the reverse.

Journalists do more than gather and report facts. They tell stories. They select and arrange facts to tell what they hope will be a story interesting enough to grab the attention of the public. As Robert Darnton points out in his convincing portrait of the ethos of the news room, "newspaper stories must fit cultural preconceptions of news."[4] The first thing a reporter does on being given an assignment is to search the newspaper's "morgue," and nowadays probably Nexis as well, to get the background and to see how the story has been handled before.

"Big stories develop in special patterns and have an archaic flavor, as if they were metamorphoses of Ur-stories that have been lost in the depths of time," writes Darnton.[5] This is true in two senses. Not only is the reporter's anticipation of the slant of a particular story influenced by how it was previously cast, but reporters in general are heavily influenced by stereotypes and preconceptions about what constitutes a good story. A good reporter is adept at recognizing and manipulating standard images, clichés, angles, and scenarios in order to call forth a conventional emotional response from the editor and the reader.

My own modest gloss on this insight into journalism is that there is a large but finite number of basic stories or plots floating around in our culture, archetypal narratives that carry wisdom and values, and that are recognized as familiar and meaningful by the reader. Americans love Cinderella stories and rags-to-riches stories and triumph-of-the-common-man stories, transfiguration narratives like "Beauty and the Beast," and stories about the lonely individual standing bravely against great odds, among many others. We never tire of the standard love story, or of retellings of King Lear or Faust, even in modern settings and even with twists. Good stories also must have believable characters, heroes and villains, conflict and resolution, and they might even carry a message: moral flaws bring down powerful and talented heroes; virtue is rewarded; hard work pays off; the world isn't fair; or pride goes before a fall. The possibilities are many but not endless. The reporter, or indeed the historian, who can fit his story into the plot lines of a familiar narrative, especially one that reinforces important cultural values, has a better chance of captivating his reader.

My visit to Hades in the spring of 1993 left me somewhat singed but also wiser in the ways of the world. As many commentators have noted, had I not been a presidential nominee, the story about me and Penn would not have generated much attention. Bringing me down was a way of embarrassing and thus weakening President Clinton. My fate was to be a voodoo doll in the hands of the President's enemies.

More important than that, however, I believe my tormentors recognized quickly that the events at Penn could be shaped to fit the critique of the university and of liberalism that already existed in the public mind, having been developed by conservative intellectuals over the previous generation. I was to be emblematic of the cultural elite that was running the country and was out of touch with the people, the elite that since the 1960s had been leading the nation away from the traditional values that made America great, that had sold out to left-wing authoritarianism, that unleashed on college campuses the NKVD of political correctness, that was the sponsor of the rise of minority groups to a privileged status within society, that was anti-Western in orientation, that was in thrall to statism, that was subversive of capitalism, and that needed to be crushed and replaced by the New Republicans. This was a role that I would have declined had I been asked, but I was imprisoned in a story someone else was telling.

As I have thought back on my experience during the spring of 1993 I have come to realize that I survived because I was able to escape from the story that had been created by the conservative masters of mass media. I could do that only when the setting shifted to the United States Senate, an arena in which face-to-face relationships are still important. There, in my old-fashioned way, I could present myself directly to the audience that was to decide my fate. I could tell my own story. Here, similarly, using the old-fashioned technology of a book, I hope to liberate myself for a final time from the grasp of netherworld narrators, and to bring back to the living earth the lessons of my painful journey.

I

The Crackpot Prez

I T ALL STARTED innocently enough in the summer of 1992. I was then halfway through my twelfth year as president of the University of Pennsylvania, and I don't think I am deluding myself by remembering that things were going extremely well. It is true that the University was facing a dense collection of prickly problems. Our state appropriation was being held up and threatened in Harrisburg, producing an uncomfortable budget squeeze. We were being sued by an advocacy group for allegedly not fulfilling our century-old obligation to provide "Mayor's Scholarships" to Philadelphia students.[1] We were negotiating with the city to acquire the civic center, which borders the campus and was critical to the expansion plans of our Medical Center. It was no longer needed by the city because of the construction of a modern convention center on Market Street East. We were also planning an ambitious cogeneration plant that the local electric company, PECO, was opposing by bringing political pressure to bear on us. All of these things together put us in a delicate political situation, making us more vulnerable than usual to the push and pull of political and economic forces in society at large. "Ivory Tower" is less and less appropriate as a metaphor for the position of the university in society.

On campus, a coalition of advocacy groups was pressing the University to dispossess the fraternities that occupied houses on Locust Walk, the pedestrian Broadway of our large but compact campus. Their point was that having the all-male, mainly white fraternities occupy such privileged space in the heart of the campus was not only unfair to women and members of minority groups who were excluded, it also communicated an unfortunate message about the University. Fraternity partisans responded that it was not their fault that the University had grown over the last hundred years, so that their houses that once had been on busy city streets on the periphery of a disparate collection of academic buildings were now on bucolic Locust Walk in the heart of a consolidated campus, and it would be unfair as well as illegal to evict them.

Other issues were swirling around. I wanted to buy the huge, empty General Electric factory building on our border even though we had no immediate need for it. A new land-use master plan was pending before the trustees, having been thoroughly debated on campus. The trustees were divided on the merits of a proposed new student center and bookstore, given such a spectacular design by Kohn Pederson Fox that it seemed sure to become a signature building. A high profile faculty/administrator/trustee "process re-engineering" task force was roaming the University looking for cost savings. Lesbians and gays were campaigning for recognition of same-sex partnerships by the University so that partners would be covered by health insurance just as spouses were. The reaction to the Rodney King jury verdict had come close to igniting the campus earlier in the year, indicating that intergroup relations were still a bit raw. With all of these matters demanding attention, I was losing one of my most able and trusted colleagues, the executive vice president, who was leaving to join an investment management firm.

Such problems, part of a different story that I do not intend to tell here, are the ever-present companions of college presidents, hardly oppressive enough to make me want to leave. Besides, there were more reasons to feel good than to cause worry. Undergraduate students were proud to be at Penn, as was I. The undergraduate program was zooming up through the *U.S. News and World Report* rankings, suspect though they may be, and was on the verge of breaking into the top ten where it was destined to settle in. Wharton, Law, Education, and Medicine in particular were on steep upward trajectories. Nursing and the Annenberg School for Communications were arguably the best of their kind in the country. Only Stanford had as many professional schools ranked in the top ten as Penn. The fund-raising campaign that was due to end in June 1994 was roaring along successfully. We were already nearing the ambitious one billion dollar goal we had set, and I was quietly confident that we would exceed the then existing record of $1.3 billion, set by Stanford University, for five-year campaigns, not bad for a campaign that was planned during the stock market crash of 1987 and was conducted during a recession.[2] More important than the dollars raised, buildings built, and faculty hired, Penn had shaken off its version of the Philadelphia disease, the feeling that it is not really as good as the best. While no one was looking, Penn had begun to think of itself in a new way.

As the academic year 1992-93 started, I had reason to feel good about things. The problem lay elsewhere. It had to do with the rhythm of an institution's life. I was approaching the end of my "work plan" for Penn. If I were to stay longer, I would need to reassess our strategic plan, produce an entirely new set of objectives for the next five years that would grow out of that reassessment, and be prepared to stay long enough to assure their success. If I did not want to make that major commitment of imagination, energy and time, I should go. The logical time for me to leave Penn would be the end of the campaign in June 1994, twenty-two months away. I had therefore already begun talking confidentially to the chairman of the trustees, Alvin Shoemaker, so we could together plan for a smooth transition.

For me, at the age of fifty-eight, this created a "what next?" problem. Flying back to Philadelphia in the middle of August from a wedding in Maine of the daughter of one of our close friends, I found myself thinking about the remarks that I would be making to freshman convocation Labor Day weekend. For twenty years, plane rides had provided a large share of the quiet time that I needed for reflection. Wedged into my seat (never in first class, of course; neither my own sense of self nor the democratic ethos of Penn would tolerate that), I was free of phone calls and meetings. This was rare unstructured time when I could read and think without feeling guilty about some pressing matter that was waiting to be tended to.

I thought that I might play upon one of my favorite themes at that convocation, one of the great paradoxes at the core of the human personality: our simultaneous desire to be valued as unique individuals and yet to be part of something bigger than we are individually. We want to be both the One and the Many. The traditional college years, eighteen to twenty-two, are typically the years when students are trying to determine who they are, to solve what Erik Erikson termed the "identity crisis." Consequently, it is a time of self-absorption and introspection, of trying on different roles and experimenting with alternative values. Yet, it is also a time of painful cliqueishness and elaborate strategies to make sure that one belongs, and even that the belonging is evident in one's appearance. As we explore our uniqueness, we are paradoxically seeking experiences of "solidarity" that reassure us that we are not alone. While we are looking inward, absorbed in the self-centered struggle to determine who we are as individuals, we are also looking outward, establishing close, trusting relationships with others. The friends we make during these years are frequently the best friends of our lives. This paradox is rich in meaning. In order to give of yourself, you need to know who you are, but you find out who you are in the act of giving yourself to others in friendship or in common enterprises. Both are true at the same time; we are both individuals and social animals. Particularly in American culture, the interplay between individualism and community is the site where each of us works out his identity.

I wanted to connect this phenomenon to public service. I had long been a booster of student volunteerism and service learning, and I was delighted that Penn had become a national model of student service. In a presidential election year, and at a time when cynics of the left and the right were attacking government as useless and inept, perhaps I could swim against the tide with a message about the duty and the rewards of public service. Thinking about how I was going to exhort the freshmen caused me to think about my own sense of duty, a strong residue of my Methodist upbringing.[3]

A couple of weeks later, back on Martha's Vineyard for a final week of vacation before the hordes descended upon the campus, I played as much golf as possible. I know that it is not politically correct to play golf, linked as it is to racial, gender, and religious intolerance, but I am a shameless enthusiast who came to the game late in life, courtesy of a bum knee that made tennis no longer much fun. An even greater complication for any hope I might entertain of posing as the simple tribune of the people is the fact that, among my golfing buddies on the Vineyard, where I have been going in the summer with my family since 1966, is Vernon Jordan, the high-profile political and corporate insider.

I had known Vernon since 1982 when his daughter graduated from Penn and he was the Commencement speaker. Aside from that pleasant experience, we also shared several things: a delight in the Vineyard, a boyhood in the South, and a dedication to racial justice. It was natural that we would get along well. Being a friend of Vernon, of course, does not distinguish me from roughly half of the American population. His astonishingly wide acquaintanceship, and his excellent judgment, make him an extremely valuable advisor and board member. When he and I talked in August 1992, he was enjoying a last rest before being engulfed in the intense post-Labor-Day presidential campaign of another of his long-time friends, Bill Clinton.

As it happened, my wife, Lucy, and I were also, in a more modest way, supporting Clinton for president. Lucy is a lawyer who has devoted her career to juvenile law and advocacy on behalf of public policies affecting children. After our youngest child, Elizabeth, reached school age, Lucy went back to school herself, finishing the final two years of her bachelor degree by going part-time to Princeton University, where I was then teaching, finishing in 1975. While I was serving as president of Tulane University, and Lucy was being the "charming-wife-of," she was also going to law school full time, receiving her J.D. in 1979 from Tulane. She started her career in New Orleans, as a staff attorney for Advocates for the Developmentally Disabled, a public-interest law group that represented people with disabilities, children among them, and worked on issues of public policy.

When I went to the University of Pennsylvania in 1981 as president, Lucy first took some time to get us settled into the new president's residence on campus and then went to work as a staff lawyer in the excellent public interest law group in Philadelphia, the Juvenile Law Center (JLC). After an eight year mutual tutorial with the remarkable founder and director of the JLC, Robert Schwartz, Lucy left in 1990 and set up a statewide research, resource, and advocacy organization, headquartered in Harrisburg, called Pennsylvania Partnerships for Children (PPC). It is a state-level version of Marion Wright Edelman's Children's Defense Fund (CDF), on whose board Lucy served. The chair of the CDF Board was Hillary Clinton.

I first saw the Clintons in action at a planning retreat for CDF held at the summer home of Laura Chasin on Chappaquidick a couple of years earlier. Bill Clinton, then Governor of Arkansas and a presidential hopeful, accompanied his wife. What impressed me about Bill Clinton then was not only his legendary warmth and intelligence, but the fact that he did not "take over" the meeting. He behaved as simply another interested observer of the Board's discussions. His wife led those discussions and was clearly in charge. That, I thought, was impressive; few of the rich and powerful with whom I dealt could have done that.

Not only did I admire that ability to play a subordinate role, but I liked the other things that I knew about Bill Clinton. He was a progressive Southern governor, liberal on race and social issues, conservative on economic and fiscal policy, and pragmatic about politics. He was a founder and leader of the Democratic Leadership Forum, a faction that was attempting to move the Democratic Party to the center of the political spectrum. In broad terms, his politics were my own. Lucy and I had contributed the maximum allowed by the law and our budget as soon as there was a Clinton Campaign organization in existence. A year later, in the fall of 1992, I joined a group of university presidents in the unusual act of endorsing Clinton for the presidency. Looking back, I am sorry I did that, not because of any judgments about Clinton's performance but because it is not a good idea for university presidents to endorse political candidates. It is fine to speak out on public issues having to do with education, and I have done that throughout my career, but engaging in partisan politics risks politicizing the university in an unhealthy way.

Nevertheless, when I was poking through the woods of the Farm Neck golf course with Vernon Jordan just before Labor Day in 1992 looking for our errant tee shots, I was already a firm supporter of Bill Clinton. At the urging of our playing companion, Don Brown, with whom I had been talking about my future, I explained my "what next?" problem to Vernon. During a previous round of golf at Farm Neck, he had told me that under no circumstances would he take a position in a Clinton administration, but I nevertheless told him that working in Washington in a Clinton administration was something that might interest me.

As usual, Vernon gave me very good advice. While acknowledging that there might be a chance for me to do something interesting in Washington, he told me to think carefully about two things. Did I want to make the financial sacrifice a tour in government would entail, and did I want to live under the heightened scrutiny that public service at my level would certainly bring? Washington was getting to be a mean place, Vernon said, implying that he was not sure that I could survive in that atmosphere. He was right to worry. Nevertheless, he said he imagined that he and Warren Christopher would be involved in the talent search, if Clinton were elected, and that he would be glad to look after my interests.

I told the Trustee Executive Committee at its September meeting that I intended to leave by June 30, 1994, and that I thought I should announce this publicly at some time between January and June 1993. The tail end of any college presidency is always tricky. On the one hand, it is desirable to provide enough public lead time for a careful search for the next president and then for a smooth transition. On the other hand, it would be good to minimize the resulting "lame duck" period of inevitably slowing rates of progress. I hoped we could get it right. The departure of the executive vice president was a blow, of course, but my chief-of-staff, John Gould, had moved over to serve as acting executive vice president while the search for a permanent EVP proceeded. John was doing extremely well in a challenging situation. I had also kept Mike Aiken, the provost, fully informed of my thinking, so I could expect him and perhaps Rick Nahm, the vice president for planning and development, to be open to job possibilities elsewhere. I worried about the appearance of my administration "unraveling." On the other hand, there were several deans who could serve as interim provost or even interim president, and the development staff was deep in talent.

The fall was packed with problems both routine and unusual; I was also teaching my undergraduate seminar on the history of the 1960s. While juggling the crammed agenda with as much of the outer appearance of inner serenity as I could muster, Lucy and I went to Korea and Japan to make connections with alumni/ae and to cultivate fund-raising possibilities. I got through the meetings of the full Board of Trustees in late October with no damage, and Lucy and I were elated when Bill Clinton won the election on November 5. I was particularly pleased that I had invited Hillary Clinton well before the election to be Penn's Commencement speaker in May 1993 whether or not her husband won the election. Lucy and I went to Washington for the CDF gala in November soon after the election. The President-elect and Hillary attended. Hillary spoke after dinner and was impressive. Lucy and I exchanged pleasantries with the Clintons at the reception, and it was interesting to discover how thrilled we both were with that simple and inconsequential event. Even though we have lived lives that have brought us into frequent contact with the rich, famous, and powerful, so that we are no longer excited by the prospect of meeting a celebrity, the aura of the American presidency affected us, just as it does most Americans.

Some time between the election and Thanksgiving, I worked up my courage and called Vernon Jordan. He and Warren Christopher were indeed deeply involved in managing the transition. At Vernon's suggestion, but without any expectations or any particular position in mind, I sent him my *curriculum vitae*, the first of several that disappeared aimlessly into the great maw of Washington. More purposefully, I wanted to get a delegation of college presidents in to see the President-elect to emphasize the importance to higher education of the student-aid programs and the research budgets administered by the National Science Foundation, the National Institutes of Health, and various cabinet departments. Indirect cost recovery on research contracts was an especially hot topic then, and I hoped we could explain its mysteries to the President-elect in a more sympathetic light than was being shed by Representative John Dingell or the daily press.

Realizing that every other organized sector with things at stake in Washington would be pressing for a similar audience, I was prepared to be shunted aside to see Johnetta Cole, the president of Spelman College who had just been named to head the transition "cluster" that included higher education. I knew Johnetta only slightly, but favorably, from our service together on the Board of the American Council on Education, the "umbrella" organization for all post-secondary education. She would be a friendly face and sympathetic voice.

Vernon told me that he would see what he could do about getting an audience of some kind for me, but he warned that my delegation could not look just like me. He meant that it could not consist entirely of white males representing elite research universities. This hint from a friend alerted me to the importance of the "politics of perception," the ruling ethos of the public world with which I was about to collide, and it made me think again of the disjunction between the way I think of myself and the thing that I sometimes symbolize to others.

With that warning tucked into my subconscious, I continued to chip away at the year's agenda for Penn, and to mull over my "what next?" problem. I had for some time been aware of a troubling proposition that applied to me. Sometimes, you cannot be the person you want to be by doing the things you want to do. In my case, there has been a contradiction between the pleasure I get from contemplative pursuits—puttering in my study, reading, thinking, writing, preparing to teach—and the satisfaction I derive from being at the center of action, preferably leading an organization toward a worthy goal. I love the process of thinking and writing, the ways in which a teacher/scholar spends his time; I don't enjoy the ways in which a college president spends most of his time, even though I love being at the center of decision making.

In addition to this unresolved conflict in my psyche, certain other personal disabilities emerged from my late-life vocational crisis. I was raised in modest circumstances in a Methodist family in Birmingham, Alabama. The virtues that I most admire were absorbed from that strict upbringing: humility, self-sacrifice, courage, determination, self-discipline, integrity, and service to others. I certainly do not claim that I always exemplify those virtues, but they are the ones by which I measure myself.

Somehow I also managed to infer from the conscious training that I got in Southern manners that they were not just empty forms, not simply gestures that marked one as belonging to a particular stratum of society, though they were that as well: giving rise to the term, "polite society." They were all based on the belief that selfishness is bad. Each of us must realize that we are not the only individuals in the world, so we have to work out ways of sharing the world with others. There are many ways of doing that, of course, but in the South of my childhood, Christianity was the unspoken paradigm: men were to defer to women, the young were to defer to the old, the able were to defer to the infirm, and the strong were to defer to the weak. Since we are all God's children in equal measure, it was not polite to do anything that would call attention to an inequality. Hip post-modernists would hasten to point out that these rituals of manners "enacted" or "performed," and thus reinforced, the prevailing patriarchal order. If this is true, it is true in an upsidedown kind of way, in a way that can only be understood in terms of the Christian paradox: Jesus as both Lord and servant. This is the opposite of the way segregation "performed" the caste subordination of blacks that was required by the dominant white Southern society. The more important function of being polite was to remind the favored of their stewardship obligations, and to remind us all of our mutual obligations to each other. Manners, like other symbolic behaviors, are not frivolous.

I can even now hear my mother speaking scornfully of particular people in Birmingham who were flamboyant self-promoters, or who seemed to be publicly self-serving. In her world, one was not supposed to put oneself forward. "If you have to blow your own horn," she repeatedly said in various ways, "there must be something wrong with the music." That contrasts with the more popular current mantra, "If you don't blow your own horn, who will?" The attitudes that I derived from my parents not only seem quaintly anachronistic in celebrity-haunted America, they may be fundamentally disabling.

One of my favorite cartoons of contemporary Washington shows the President and another man standing in the Oval Office. They are looking out the French doors. The visitor says, "Beautiful sunset." The President says, "Thank you." The connection between what one does and what one takes credit for, never very strong in politics, is weakening as attention spans shorten, news cycles speed up, and the manipulation of public perceptions gets more sophisticated.

I have seen this trend at work in my own field. When I began at Tulane my eighteen-year career of being a college president, even while believing in, and using, participatory decision making, we always tried to keep the long-term good of the university as the policy objective. After the consultive process had produced that policy, then we turned our attention to the task of explaining it to the various audiences (students, parents, alumni, trustees, faculty, staff, the higher education community, and the general public). Increasingly, I think, decision makers ask simply, "What can we explain successfully to our various audiences? That is what we will do." It is a short step from that to merely communicating instead of acting, substituting image for substance. This is easy enough to grasp in theory, but I find it unnatural and very difficult to put into practice.

My career is a good example of the aphorism that life is what happens to you when you are planning something else. The "something else" that I was planning was to teach history at the college level and be a scholar. I was very naive about what that life was actually like, and especially about how to prepare myself for it, but I benefited from some amazing good fortune.

As an undergraduate at Vanderbilt University, my love of history was stimulated and encouraged by an excellent history faculty. Their lives looked pleasant enough to me, so I decided to become a teacher. First, however, I owed three years of service to the Navy because I was at Vanderbilt on an NROTC scholarship. I spent those three years, 1956-59, on the *USS James C. Owens* (DD-776), a World War II era destroyer based in Norfolk, but usually at sea. That was a totally absorbing experience that I did not so much enjoy as find fascinating and rewarding. Nowhere else could I have gotten so much responsibility while so young, and come into contact with men from vastly different backgrounds from my own. Toward the end of my time aboard the *Owens*, I got a letter from the Office of Naval Personnel offering me the chance to teach at Annapolis if I would extend my service for two years. By then, I was married and had one child and very little money, and I thought that it would be a great idea to have a two-year transition to civilian life at full pay, the glorious sum of thirty-five hundred dollars per year. Besides, teaching history would be a good way to learn and to prepare for graduate school.

When I arrived at the United States Naval Academy in the summer of 1959, I was shocked to discover that my promise as a scholar had somehow gone unnoticed, and I had been assigned to the Weapons Department. I went hesitantly to see the Captain who was the head of the Weapons Department and explained that I thought I might be able to make a bigger contribution to the USNA in the English, History, and Government Department, called the "bull" department in Academy parlance, revealing a particular view of the hierarchy of knowledge. "Nonsense," said the Captain, with the certainty of military command, "Bull professors are a dime a dozen. What we need is a gunnery officer fresh from the fleet to help shape up these midshipmen."

I therefore spent the next two years during daylight hours drilling midshipmen in the operational niceties of naval gunnery, anti-submarine warfare, and the theory of surface-to-air and air-to-air missiles. On a couple of nights a week, I went into Washington and took history courses in the evening division of American University.

Occasionally I drew weekend duty and would have to chaperone the afternoon dances arranged for first-year midshipmen, called Plebes. The dances at tea time were therefore known as "Plebe Tea Fights." Bus loads of young ladies from area colleges would arrive at the entrance to cavernous Dahlgren Hall, home of both the Weapons Department and the scheduled "vertical wrestling matches." Disgorged from the buses, groups of young ladies would come down the broad stairway onto the huge gym floor. Plebes were herded behind a rope to one side. Outside the rope stood an upperclassman from the committee in charge of the event. He would size up each young woman descending the stairs in her proper 1950s tea dance outfit, reach into the milling herd behind the rope, grab a Plebe of the proper height, and propel him out to escort that particular guest. A surprising number of marriages came out of this system.

Now, it happened that the leading historian of the South, and the man I most wanted to study with in graduate school, C. Vann Woodward, was on the faculty of the Johns Hopkins University, not very far up the road in Baltimore. It also happened that Lucy's parents, Clifford and Virginia Durr, had known Professor Woodward since he was a graduate student at Chapel Hill writing *Tom Watson, Agrarian Rebel*. On one of my mother-in-law's visits to Annapolis, she arranged for us to go up and have tea with Vann and his wife, Glenn. The conversation was pleasant, though I was pretty much dumbstruck in the presence of the great man. Professor Woodward eventually excused himself from the group and told me to follow him into his study, where he quizzed me about my background and my interests. He told me that he was about to move to Yale University and that I should be sure to apply there. I did so, and I was admitted, although without a fellowship. I would be paying my own way.

As I was rejected at Hopkins, Harvard, and Princeton, I suspected that Professor Woodward had used his influence to get me in. Years later, he confirmed this suspicion when he was introducing me as the keynote speaker at a conference of history teachers. He went on to say that when he finally got to Yale, a year after I had arrived, since he had a Guggenheim fellowship that provided a year for research, he approached the Chairman, John Blum, and asked, "How is my boy Hackney doing?" John Blum said, "It's OK, Vann. You'll get the hang of Yale standards after you've been here a while." I persevered. Eventually I figured out what the study of history was about, and Vann's gamble was vindicated when my dissertation won the prize as the best in American history at Yale in 1966.

In my fourth year at Yale, when I was in the midst of writing that dissertation on the Populist and Progressive political movements in Alabama between 1890 and 1910, Professor Woodward called me to his office. He said that Princeton University was looking for someone in American history and he was sending me down. That is the way it was done in 1965. I went down, gave a talk to the department about my dissertation, met the senior Americanists individually, and had lunch with a large group of historians. Not having used the wrong fork, I was offered the job before I left campus that day. Woodward's imprimatur was powerful.

Even though we remained good friends until his death in December 1999, I think Vann never really forgave me for becoming an administrator. It was a great waste of his investment in making me a good historian. I can only plead that it happened inadvertently.

Having three children, a lot of debt from graduate school, and the magnificent salary of eighty-five hundred dollars per year, I couldn't afford to spend the summers doing research and advancing my scholarly career. My first summer at Princeton, 1966, I taught in a summer institute for high school history teachers run by Robert Lively, who had taken an interest in me because I was a discussion leader (a "preceptor" in Princeton lingo) in his large lecture course, and because I was also from his hometown of Birmingham, Alabama. The second summer, 1967, I taught in the Princeton Cooperative School Program, an Upward Bound program for disadvantaged high school boys, mostly black, from the inner cities of New Jersey. The director was a good friend, John Flemming, from Arkansas by way of Sewanee and then graduate school at Princeton, who was also just starting out on a career that has led him to being one of the world's leading scholars of medieval literature. In 1968, he passed the directorship of PCSP on to me. After taking it through the summer, I convinced the University to install Earl Thomas as the full-time, non-faculty director of PCSP, providing administrative stability and excellent leadership for a long time into the future.

About the same time, I was startled one day when the door to my basement office in McCosh Hall[4] burst open and there stood Lawrence Stone, the great British historian who had arrived at Princeton in 1963. He could be blunt and intimidating, but he was also enormously generous with his time and his help to younger colleagues, including me. "I have just come from Nassau Hall," he announced. "They want me to become the chairman of the department. I made it a condition that you be the assistant chairman. Will you do it?" It was more a command than a question, so for the next few years I did much of the scutwork of the department while Lawrence transformed a good department into a great one. I learned a lot by watching and listening to Lawrence; he ranks alongside Vann Woodward as my academic hero and model.

I remember walking across the campus one day in the spring of 1968 when I encountered President Robert Goheen heading back toward Nassau Hall. He stopped me and said that he had been trying to reach me because he wanted to talk to me. I was startled to think that he knew who I was. Furthermore, I was young enough to think that when the principal sends for you it isn't going to be good.

On the other hand, a summons from the President might have meant anything in those days because remarkable things were happening at Princeton. The revolution was in full cry. A faculty committee chaired by Gardner Patterson was doing a careful study of the likely impact of coeducation, a study that provided the factual support for President Goheen's successful argument to the trustees that coeducation would be cost efficient, would attract more and better male applicants, and would in other ways improve Princeton. The trustees agreed and decided to allow the admission of women as undergraduate students the following year. At the same time, Professor Stan Kelly and a faculty/student committee, on which I served, were working on a report that would make the governance of Princeton much more consultative. The system of selective eating clubs was under attack from within the student body. Various impolite voices disrupted the collegial calm from time to time about the war in Vietnam and racial justice at home. It was a great time to be alive and to be at Princeton.

As I walked with the President to his office in Nassau Hall, he explained that he thought the University had to respond in some way to the demands for more recognition in the curriculum of the experience of black Americans. It was not clear to him what needed to be done, nor that the faculty would approve any significant steps that might be suggested, but he was committed to supporting a serious consideration of various alternatives. It was bound to be controversial, but he wondered if I would be willing to chair a committee on the subject.

That President Goheen was turning to a junior member of the History department might have seemed a little ominous. It never occurred to me, however, that I might have been picked to be point man of this skirmish line because I was expendable. Being young and foolish, I was flattered. There were, after all, benign explanations for my being put in charge of this project. I am a specialist in the history of the American South, which is inherently about blacks and whites and their relationships to each other. Revealingly, there was no one else on the Princeton faculty whose field was more centrally concerned with the black experience. In the supercharged atmosphere of that time, my being white made it more difficult for me to be taken seriously by black students or by black activists and scholars outside the University. However, there was no choice on that account. Princeton had no black faculty member, other than the economist, Sir Arthur Lewis, and this was not his thing.

So, the committee was appointed. We spent the summer gathering information about what other institutions were doing and constructing a reading list of available scholarship. One of the quiet objections to doing anything was that, however legitimate the subject, there simply wasn't enough scholarship to support a serious intellectual effort. The mere heft of the committee's bibliography refuted that argument.

The major fault line within the committee, and among the faculty in general, distinguished between a department and an interdepartmental program. That question occupied a good bit of the committee's vigorous discussions during the academic year 1968-69. I will not rehearse those arguments here. The committee eventually chose to recommend an interdepartmental program. I believed then, and continue to believe, that in the Princeton context, that was a crucial and wise decision.

Nor will I plod through the politics of winning the approval of the faculty for a new program in Afro-American (now African American) Studies. Approval was not a foregone conclusion, even with the support of President Goheen and Provost William Bowen. Suffice it to say that we succeeded. We cobbled together a sufficient number of related courses already on the books which, with the addition of a couple of new courses, presented a respectable beginning of an effort to include the experience of African Americans throughout the humanities and social sciences at Princeton.

By the time the faculty brought the program into legal existence, it was clear that we did not have adequate faculty to lead the program or to sustain real scholarly inquiry over a long period of time. I served as the acting director of the program through its first year of existence while we recruited a permanent director.

Then, in the wake of the Cambodian incursion, in the spring of 1970, when the dormant anti-war movement was awakened with disturbing fervor, I was asked by the administration to set up a draft counseling office where students could have their options and legal obligations explained. This was a situation that made me very uneasy, though I understood the University's desire to be as responsive as possible to legitimate student needs and desires. I was opposed to the war, but I was not in favor of draft resistance. My own Southern sense of honor would have required me to accept a draft call even though I was against the war. On the other hand, I also thought that every eligible man deserved to know what rights and options he had within the system so he could make up his own mind about what to do. I proceeded on that basis. I was the chair of the local ACLU, so I easily found my way to qualified counselors in the region and arranged for them to staff a center in a university building where students could go for information. It was the policy of the center, of course, that there would be no advocacy of draft resistance, and so far as I know there was none.

As the unpaid faculty overseer of this activity, I was one of the people consulted by the Princeton undergraduates who organized a chapter of what became the Union of National Draft Organizations (UNDO). That summer, UNDO called a national meeting in Princeton. Hundreds of politically engaged college students would be coming to our picture-postcard college town. Where would they stay? There was certainly no room at the Nassau Inn. My wife and her friends, with enormous effort, enlisted scores of sympathetic Princeton faculty and townspeople who were willing to house groups of visiting UNDO students. However, when those students arrived in Princeton for the rally, hirsute and unkempt, they would have nothing to do with bourgeois hospitality. They brought their sleeping bags, guitars, and recreational substances, and they sprawled together on the soccer fields of Princeton, saving many a neat, clean, wholesome Princeton home from certain depredation.

I was on sabbatical leave during the academic year 1970-71, spending a good bit of time on the road doing research on the Civil Rights Movement. When I returned to full-time teaching in 1971-72, the mood on campus had swung dramatically toward quiescence. This was the period when the commune movement was roaring along. Young people disillusioned by the supposedly ineffectual attempts to change society through direct confrontation or through politics decided to build intentional communities that would live by alternative values, thus converting the world to a better way of life by demonstrating the superiority of cooperative values.

This was also Bob Goheen's last year of a remarkable presidency that had transformed Princeton. To the surprise of very few, the Trustees turned to his provost, William Bowen, to become the next president of Princeton. That winter, President-elect Bowen asked me to meet him after a basketball game, a considerate bit of timing in that we were both Princeton basketball fanatics. I don't remember who won the game that night, but I do remember that

Bill asked me to take his place as provost when he moved into the president's office that summer.

As Lucy and I talked about it that night and the next day, I realized that I was spending a lot of my time doing administrative chores of one kind or another, while also teaching and publishing. I constantly felt torn, pulled in different directions. Perhaps a stint as a full-time administrator would allow me to discover whether I liked that better than full-time teaching and writing. If I didn't like it, I could always return to the faculty after five years and not be much the worse for wear. The new administration was especially rich in talent. I learned a lot from my colleagues, and I particularly learned from Bill Bowen, a remarkable academic leader.[5]

Unfortunately, in my third year as provost, the fall of 1974, before I had a definitive answer to the question of which university track I wished to run on, I got a call from Edmund McIlhenny who was chairman of the Tulane University Board of Administrators, that is, the trustees. He was looking for a new president and had been told that I might fit Tulane's needs.

The lure of the South was great. If I were going to remain in administration, being president of a first-tier private university would allow me to make a contribution to my native region, a region that suffered then even more than it does now from an educational deficit. The universe of first-rate private universities in the South is extremely small. It consists of Duke, Vanderbilt, Tulane, and Emory, with Rice as a special case. Tulane, I eventually decided, was an opportunity that I could not pass up.

I labored five years in New Orleans in a tough environment, what in the business world would be called "a turnaround situation." Tulane's trajectory changed dramatically. I earned the usual number of enemies for doing what was necessary, and I made some mistakes that exacerbated the inevitable friction. When Penn came looking for a president to succeed Martin Meyerson, I was therefore receptive. The Tulane and Penn stories await a different telling. For current purposes, I need only note that when I moved to Penn in February 1981, I found myself in the middle of a huge controversy because the trustees had selected me rather than the inside favorite, Vartan Gregorian.

At Tulane, I had arrived as the exotic ivy leaguer, full of mystery and magic. At Penn, it was assumed by campus activists, the student newspaper, and the local press that I must be the opposite of Greg. After all, our appearances differ. He was short, plump, swarthy, charming, and ebullient; I was tall, slender, white, and reserved. Since he was liberal and creative, I must be conservative and managerial. Charisma is in the eye of the beholder. Given my later public persona, it is ironic that I spent the 1980s fencing with the "progressive" activists at Penn, who cast me as the oppressive representative of corporate America. It took me perhaps four years to break through those stereotypes completely and establish warm relationships with the dominant political center of faculty and students.

The point of this race through my resume is that, after applying to graduate school, I never had to hustle or to promote myself to get my next job. They came to me. This created a hazard of good fortune. Here I was in the winter of 1992-93, faced with a "what next?" problem of large proportions, without a lot of experience in finding jobs for myself, especially in Washington. I was therefore not surprised to notice shortly before Christmas that the Clinton cabinet had been filled without me. I was at least clever enough to realize that if I wanted to go to Washington, reticence was not going to work. On the other hand, I didn't have a particular job in mind, and I didn't know how to pursue it, even if I knew what I wanted.

Then, on December 2, I read in the newspaper that Lynne Cheney had resigned as Chair of the National Endowment for the Humanities, to become effective January 20, 1993, the day President Clinton would be inaugurated. Nothing could have made her political conception of the job more apparent. Ignoring that storm warning, I thought to myself, "Hmmm, that is a job I could do. It might even be fun." I realized that I was at a great disadvantage in the behind-the-scenes maneuvering for jobs in the new administration. I did not even hear the gossip. So, I called Joe Watkins, who had been one of my assistants at Penn, and who had gone to Washington to work in the Bush administration. He was on his way back to the Philadelphia area with the hope of finding a way to run for public office as a Republican. He made an effort in the Republican primary for U.S. Senator, but the odds were too long. The Republicans missed a terrific candidate.

Joe dropped by Eisenlohr, the president's house on the campus, in late December, bringing me the "Plum Book," which lists all the appointive offices in the federal government, along with a lot of good advice about how to maneuver. He also reported that he had sent my *c.v.* to the Clinton transition office in the hands of a friend of his who is a Democrat, with the message that I would make a good chair of the NEH. I had also just learned that, without my asking, Judge Leon Higginbotham, a Penn trustee, had sent a letter on my behalf to Vernon Jordan. Joe's advice was to flood the office with as many pieces of paper as possible. Chaos being the rule in such operations, you could never tell when a *c.v.* or a letter of recommendation would find itself in the right pile of papers at the right time to get one on a list of prospects. After his tutorial, I remember thinking that I was probably in the process of being humbled.

Lucy and I took our family, eleven in all, including children, in-laws, and grandchildren, to Club Med in Ixtappa, Mexico in early January for a wonderful week of sun and fun together. I went to the convention of the American Council on Education in San Diego when we returned. There I had a long talk with Tom Ehrlich, a close friend since we had worked side by side at Penn during my first five years, when he was provost, before he went to be the president of Indiana University. He was leaving IU now, so we had a lot to discuss about our futures. He had decided that he didn't want to do another university presidency, though there were a couple of great ones pursuing him. He and Ellen were headed back to Palo Alto to lead a more civilized existence near their children. When I told him that I was a bit at a loss to know how to pursue the NEH chairmanship, he told me that I should call Joe Duffy, who Tom thought was the most wired-in person in Washington. Joe was then the president of American University, though he soon joined the Clinton administration as the director of USIA. I had known him for some time. In addition, he could tell me something about the NEH; he had served a term as chairman as the appointee of President Jimmy Carter.

I called Joe in late January, not long after I got back from San Diego. He was extremely nice and very helpful. By then I knew that one of the pieces of paper with my name on it had fluttered onto the right stack in the right office at the right time and that my name had once been somewhere on a long list of people being considered for the NEH. David Morse, Penn's excellent director of federal relations, had called John Hammer, director of the National Humanities Alliance, the coalition of scholarly and public organizations that benefit from NEH grants, and learned that my name was not being pursued because it was thought that I was not interested. I told Joe Duffy this bit of gossip, and he promised to find out what the state of play was, and also to pass on the word that I really would be interested.

This was after the Inauguration, so the appointment process was now being handled by Bruce Lindsey's Office of Presidential Personnel, and the transition team had melted away. David Morse had also been able to construct a list of "mentions," people whose names were being unofficially circulated as possibilities among various interested organizations in order to gauge the possible reception of their nomination. There were nine on David's list, and

I knew seven of them relatively well, and they were all attractive candidates. The good news here was that it was not yet done; I was not too late.

Bolstered by this information, on January 29 I called Senator Harris Wofford, whom I had known since his days as president of Bryn Mawr College. I asked him if he could help me, assuming that he did not have another horse in the race. He was immediately supportive. Not only did he not have another candidate for the NEH, but his candidate for Secretary of Education had not been picked, and he thought Clinton needed to appoint some people from the big industrial states like Pennsylvania that had supported him. It sounded like a good argument to me. I began to practice my Rocky imitation, though it usually comes out sounding more like the southside in Birmingham than south Philly.

Harris said he would go all out for me. He then advised me to get as many endorsements as possible from influential folks, politicians and others. We went over some names. He urged me to get Marion Wright Edelman to speak to Hillary for me. I said that if I approached it right, I could probably get Lucy to speak to Hillary as well. I was beginning to get the hang of this thing.

I was also getting excited about what I could do at the NEH. Joe Duffy had told me that it was more of a day-to-day management job than people realized, a useful warning because Bill Bennett and Lynne Cheney had turned it into a conservative pulpit. I remember thinking at about this time that I had great respect for what the NEH did; I thought I could do the internal management of the agency, the politics of the humanities community, the lobbying of Congress, and still have time and energy to perform as a depoliticized spokesperson for the humanities in American life, and to help the NEH create some exciting new programs.

Harris's follow-through was impressive. He called Bruce Lindsey immediately. I am sure he had a number of things to take up with

Lindsey, but he also put in a word for me. I also got busy. I called Philadelphia Congressmen Tom Foglietta and Bill Gray; both were supportive. Bill Gray, a member of the Democratic leadership in the House, called Bruce Lindsey on my behalf. I began to ask other friends, like Robert Brustein, director of the American Repertory Theater at Harvard, to write to Lindsey about me.

Meanwhile, Mike Aiken and Rick Nahm let me know that they were about to be selected to head other institutions, Mike to be chancellor of the University of Illinois, Champaign-Urbana, and Rick to become president of Knox College in Galesburg, Illinois. I had contingency plans ready. After appropriate consultations, I would name Marvin Lazerson, dean of the School of Education, to act as provost, and I would simply promote Ginny Clark, associate V.P. for Development and Alumni Relations, to succeed Rick. There was, however, a timing problem presented by the search for the new executive vice president (EVP). I could not really announce that I planned to step down on June 30, 1994, until the EVP had been named. Naturally, I would have to tell that person what was about to happen, and that would make the selling of the job a little harder.

My dual life was far from boring, as a reconstruction of February 3, 1993, indicates. My day started at 8:30 A.M. with a briefing of a large group of trustees by our financial team on a "sources and uses" analysis of University finances, tracing more clearly than ever before where our revenues came from and how they flowed within the institution. That meeting dissolved into a meeting of the Trustees' special Long Range Planning Committee where Bill Kelley, the dean of the medical school and CEO of the medical center, successfully presented his strategic plan for the medical center. Those crucial discussions occupied the morning. Between 2 and 3 P.M., I conferred with the general counsel, Shelley Green, and the vice provost for research, Barry Cooperman, about a suit against the University by a company accusing our faculty of leaking its trade secrets about solid-state batteries. Between 4 and 5 P.M., Mike Aiken and I met with the faculty senate executive committee, about a committee report recommending changes in the "just cause" procedures, the process through which faculty members can be disciplined, which had just failed miserably to handle a case of faculty plagiarism. I spent the evening, from 6 P.M. to 10 P.M. at the annual football banquet, which was very upbeat.

During the little empty spaces in the day, especially between 3 and 4 P.M., I did my telephoning. Among my calls that day was one from Harris Wofford, who reported that he had talked to Bruce Lindsey again and that Bruce had said that my name was on a short list for the NEH. He also assured Harris, with what I imagine was a bit of exasperation, that, yes, he understood how distinguished I was. I remember thinking at this point how frustrating it was to be working in the dark; no one from the White House had gotten in touch with me to make an assessment of how well I might be expected to do the job. I had no chance to speak for myself. It also felt strange to know that the White House's ultimate selection would be heavily influenced by political consideration, what constituency or person it wanted to please, and what message might be communicated by the selection of a particular person. My value, initially at least, was purely symbolic. I could only line up my support and hope for the best.

I left the next day for an alumni speaking engagement and fund-raising excursion in Florida. Lucy was in Montgomery caring for her mother after an operation to repair a broken hip, so I traveled alone. I spent a delightful evening on Key Biscayne in the home of Carlos and Rosa de la Cruz; Carlos was a Penn alumnus who had been extremely successful in business. Ironically, Carlos and Rosa, whom I do not think of as arrogant, left-wing elitists, collect the work of Andres Serrano, the Latino artist whose "Piss Christ" ignited one of the most ferocious attacks by Jesse Helms and the religious right on funding for the National Endowment for the Arts.

After my work was done, I went up the coast to spend the rest of the weekend with Don and Ann Brown at their place at Frenchman's Creek. Ann, an active consumer advocate, was waging a quiet campaign for appointment to be chair of the Consumer Products Safety Commission. We had fun swapping stories about the process. She also was successful in her quest and was a brilliant success in the job.

I returned to Philadelphia that Monday, February 8, to find some messages from David Morse who had been trolling for information in Washington. He reported that John Hammer had been asked by the White House whether there were any negatives about me in the humanities community. We don't see the wind; we just see the ripples on the water.

The next bit of hearsay evidence was provided by a call on February 12 from Jackie Trescott, the reporter on the culture beat for the *Washington Post*, who was pursuing a list of seven possible nominees for the chairmanship of the NEH. I could only tell her that the White House had not been in touch with me. Shortly afterward, someone from Bruce Lindsey's office called my office and asked that my *c.v.* be sent to them, yet another paper missile fired into the dark void of Washington. David Morse guessed that they were delaying a choice for the NEH hoping to be able to announce the NEH and NEA together. If there were a woman for the NEA, and all the rumored candidates were women, that would provide some camouflage if the NEH went to a white male. I understood that.

On March 3, the *Washington Post* reported that I was the leading candidate for chairmanship of the NEH. This was news to me, albeit good news. It also began to make my situation mildly uncomfortable. Rumors were swirling about. The *Chronicle of Higher Education* sent a photographer to take my picture, saying they would save it for an appropriate occasion. Stan Katz at the American Council of Learned Societies, my friend and later my close ally, was telling people that I was about to be nominated. Harris Wofford called to say that he had talked to Hillary about me and that she was enthusiastic. Charley Pizzi at the Philadelphia Chamber of Commerce told me that he had heard it was to be announced that week. The *Daily Pennsylvanian* called me for a reaction because they had it from an unimpeachable source in the White House that I was to have been announced the preceding Friday. I could not react to something that had not been announced, nor could I explain why it had not been announced. Neither could the reporter. This state of suspended animation had its amusing aspects. Students would fall into step with me on Locust Walk and ask brightly, "Have you gotten the job yet?" Others would just say, "Good luck," as they passed. Worry about being a publicly rejected suitor was the major discomfort at this point.

Lucy and I went to Montgomery, Alabama the weekend of April 2-4 where I gave the annual Durr Lecture at Auburn University in Montgomery, an event that celebrated the life and work of Lucy's father, Clifford J. Durr. My talk began by examining an apparent paradox, one of my favorite devices because I believe paradoxes expose the problem areas of cultures, and thus they can yield very interesting insights into the culture. I have been thinking about paradoxes and using them analytically for a long time, and I continue to be fascinated with them. In this case, I observed that the new globalism was begetting tribalism. It is a curious fact that the shrinking of the world under the influence of modern transportation, information technology, and the integration of economies was accompanied by an epidemic of sectarian violence. The closer we get to each other, the more we fight one another. This phenomenon, I argued, should make Americans think more carefully about what values and commitments were strong enough to hold our racially, ethnically, religiously, linguistically, culturally diverse society together. This was a theme I had pursued before, used for my remarks at Commencement in May 1993, and one that I would return to later at the NEH.

The next day, Friday, April 2, when Lucy and I were staying with my brother, Morris, and his wife, Brenda, in Birmingham, I was run to earth by Bill Gilcher, who was phoning on behalf of the Office of Presidential Personnel. Could I come talk to them next week? I said that I thought that I might be able to work that into my schedule.

Actually, it was not easy because Cokie Roberts and her mother, Lindy Boggs, were going to be on campus as Pappas Fellows that week. They were personal friends of ours and I wanted to be there during their visit. So, I could not visit Washington until Friday, April 9. I rode down on the train in high spirits the evening before. Cokie and Lindy had been a wonderful team. Cokie was brash and irreverent; her mother as usual was so sweet that you had to listen very closely to get the wisdom that she was dispensing about public life in Washington. They are so different, yet they are clearly devoted to each other. Large student audiences loved them.

In addition to that reason for feeling good, I thought that I was at last going to learn where the search for a NEH chair was. Silly me! I had spent many late night hours during that week filling out personal information forms sent by the White House, covering finances, jobs, organizational affiliations, club memberships, and residences over an impossibly long period of time. I thought that they probably would not require me to do such an onerous chore if they were not serious about me, but I was not sure.

After checking into the Hay-Adams, across the park from the White House, I met Martha Chowning in the lobby. She was the lone Clinton political appointee at the NEH, so she was to brief me on the current state of the agency. It was then functioning under Lynne Cheney's choice as acting chair, Jerry Martin, a former political appointee who had "burrowed" into a senior civil service position at the NEH.

Martin eventually left the NEH and became the first president of the American Council of Trustees and Alumni (ACTA), an organization started by Lynne Cheney, with a founding board full of high-profile public figures, including Democratic Senator Joe Lieberman (of whom, more later). The ostensible purpose of ACTA is to hold universities accountable for protecting free speech on campus, and for teaching students the fundamental values of Western Civilization. That is the way that it describes itself, but it rests more specifically upon a consistent right-wing critique of higher education that has been developed and elaborated over the past fifteen years.[6] I became the symbol of the "liberal elite" that is alleged by the right wing to be running American universities, and that is at work undermining the traditional values on which our culture depends. If this sounds to you like a conspiracy theory, you have been paying attention.

A quick flash forward can reveal this critique at work in the report released in December 2001 by ACTA, "Defending Civilization: How Our Universities are Failing America and What Can Be Done About It."[7] The report begins by noting that the country responded with admirable patriotism to the terrorism of September 11, 2001. "Not so in academe. . . . professors across the country sponsored teach-ins that typically ranged from moral equivocation to explicit condemnations of America." The report's evidence consists of 115 brief quotations from speakers on college campuses, ripped out of context, that say such things as "revenge is not justifiable"; "stop the violence, stop the hate"; "an eye for an eye makes the world blind"; as well as such dangerous truisms as that we need to understand how America is viewed by the rest of the world. The report concludes that colleges are "short on patriotism." "The message of much of academe was clear: blame America first." The technique here is quite familiar. Point to a few outlandish examples that suit your purpose, and then act as if they are typical of the whole rather than marginal. The thing to note, I believe, is that the report does not engage the dissenting ideas themselves. It simply implies that all of higher education is unpatriotic.

Why would an organization dedicated to free speech on campus attack higher education for permitting free speech? It is enough to make one suspect that the authors of the report don't want free speech; they want their speech. This is only one of a number of curiosities. Why, with President George Bush's approval ratings hovering around 92 percent, was it thought important to coerce the last 8 percent into line? Indeed, in an era of Republican hegemony, when political scientists who measure such things report that the political spectrum has shifted markedly to the right and is increasingly polarized between centrists and the right wing, do culture warriors speak in such apocalyptic terms about a liberal conspiracy to subvert the republic? The solution to these curiosities is that the ACTA report is not about rallying support in the current crisis; it is about furthering its long-term project of de-legitimizing higher education in the public mind, and advancing the world view of movement conservatives.

Meanwhile, back on April 8, 1993, I was still innocent of the covert actions and dirty tricks of the people who saw me as a convenient representative of their conspiracy theory. Martha Chowning, however, gave me an astute analysis of the internal politics of the NEH, and also handed over to me a load of NEH publications and a briefing book that told me everything anyone could want to know about the NEH and its programs. Things were beginning to look serious.

I got over to the Old Executive Office Building the next morning a little before eight, only to find that my name had not been entered into the security computer. Was this a subtle message? I was rescued from this purgatory by Leslie Maddin who happened by and recognized me. She is the daughter of a retired Penn faculty member, and she was then working in the Office of Presidential

Personnel, though in a different area from the one interested in me. She quickly found Bill Gilcher and Susan Reichly, and they all took me over to the White House Mess, where Jan Piercy met us for breakfast.

We had an interesting conversation about the NEH and the other cultural agencies. After a very long time, I finally asked, "Am I going to get the nomination?" "Oh, yes," they laughed, "we thought you knew." I suppose I should have understood that Jackie Trescott was the White House messenger.

As David Morse had guessed, they had been trying to hold the NEH until the NEA and the Institute for Museum Services were also ready to announce. They finally realized that those decisions were so indefinite that they should go ahead with the NEH—but going ahead did not really mean going ahead. They normally did not announce an "intention to nominate" until after the FBI background check. In this case, however, they would try to get Bruce Lindsey to approve going public before the check was completed. Furthermore, I would have to be cleared by the general counsel of the White House. That would take about an hour of conversation with a lawyer after he had studied my personal data. A quick telephone call revealed that the general counsel had not received the forms that I had sent by Federal Express the day before.

I explained that my situation was increasingly uncomfortable on the campus. The *Washington Post* had reported on Thursday, the previous day, that my nomination was a "done deal." A *Daily Pennsylvanian* reporter and photographer had ambushed me in 30th Street Station that evening as I was setting forth for Washington. It was very clever of them to figure out exactly what was going on. That picture and a story about my job interview in Washington appeared in the *DP* on Friday, even as I was eating breakfast in the White House Mess with the President's headhunters. Furthermore, the *New York Times* had reported that same morning, Friday, that the White House was poised to announce my nomination. It would be good for me if the President's intentions were public information so I could be definitive in announcing my own plans. They understood this, but they couldn't promise anything.

I got back to Philly at 1 P.M. and was met by a university car that took me directly out to Kennett Square, near the Penn Veterinary School's campus for large-animal medicine, to talk about Penn's appropriation with State Representative Joe Pitts, the ranking minority member of the Appropriations Committee. He was, as always, very supportive. By the time I got back to my office on campus, about 3:45, the White House General Counsel's Office had called to get my telephone numbers. They now had the forms and would be calling me. Before that could happen, however, about 4:30, Bill Gilcher called to say that at 5 P.M. the White House was going to announce the President's "intention to nominate" me. Late afternoon on a Friday, I realized later, is the traditional time to make announcements that one hopes will be seen by as few people as possible. Nevertheless, I was delighted.

A few of my close advisors assembled later that afternoon to figure out what I could and should say in public.[8] That was relatively easy: "I am delighted to be chosen and, if confirmed, will be honored to serve." I would then have to say to the university community that the trustees and I had given much thought to contingency plans and more would be announced about those shortly. Then I picked up Lucy and we caught a train for New York where we were to attend a large dinner party that evening that was part of the fund-raising campaign. The easy part of getting to Washington was over; the nightmare would soon begin.

2

THE NIGHTMARE BEGINS

T HE NIGHTMARE BEGAN the following Thursday morning, April 15, 1993. A number of black students, leaving angry notes signed "The Black Community," took 14,000 copies of the *DP* out of their free distribution racks around campus. Black students, staff, and faculty had been angry with the *DP* for some time, accusing it of being insensitive and unbalanced in its coverage of the black community at Penn. I was not aware of it at the time, but confiscating the student newspaper had become a frequently used tactic around the country by groups with a grievance.

It was not even an entirely new phenomenon at Penn. In 1987, someone in the Wharton School administration absconded with all of the *DP*s in the distribution racks in Steinberg-Dietrich, the main Wharton building. An important group of alumni was visiting Wharton that particular day, and the *DP* in its great tradition of adversarial journalism had prominently featured on the front page a scandal involving a Wharton faculty member. On that occasion, I issued a stern warning that interfering with freedom of the press would not be tolerated. On another occasion, after the *DP* had turned its special reunion edition into a roundup of the year's most negative stories, the chairman of the trustees had suggested to the student editor, whom he encountered among the reunion tents, that the editor could stuff the paper into one of his bodily orifices. It was not dignified, but I loved him for it.

By 1993, I had fought my own way to peace of mind about the *DP*, a tough struggle given the fact that the editor who assumed office soon after I arrived announced that the *DP* was the only moral voice at Penn and that it would tirelessly expose the immorality of the administration. Under his editorship and several that followed, the *DP* became very good at ferreting out scandal in the administration—whether scandal existed or not. Whenever I chided *DP* editors about getting some story wrong, they would reply that the paper regularly won top honors among college newspapers nationally. I pointed out that the judges were rewarding them for producing a well-written and interesting paper, but the judges had no idea whether the information in the paper was true or not. Nevertheless, over the years I discovered that the negative and sensationalist bent of the *DP* did not affect my standing with students or hinder the progress the University was making. Students seemed able to apply their own correctives to the paper's bias. I was about to learn, however, that the outside world did not have the same sort of filtering mechanism.

So, when each year's front-page announcement of the tuition increase was accompanied by a photograph of me from the *DP*'s archive smiling broadly as if I were enjoying gouging the students and their families, I simply thought of myself as being in on the joke. I tried to get my revenge in satirical speeches that the editors allowed me to give to the annual *DP* banquet in January. I remember in particular a skit in which I intoned a laudatory speech about the *DP* in my most florid presidential rhetoric, while the amplified off-stage voice of my assistant, Tony Marx, translated the pablum phrases into the insulting subtext. Despite the jousting, which I secretly enjoyed, I noticed that an unusual number of *DP* editors took my seminar on the history of the 1960s. When they weren't beating up on me, they were terrific young folks.

A more serious problem was that there had never been many black student reporters or writers on the *DP*. Some slight progress had been made from time to time, but not sustained. There were no black reporters or editors in 1992 or 1993, but there was a black columnist, Maceo Grant, who wrote regularly about the lack of respect black students felt they received at Penn. The provost and I had encouraged the editors during our informal conversations with them over the years to do something about this situation, and we had advised them that simply waiting for black students to respond to the general invitation to students to try out for staff positions would probably not be enough. Many black students felt like intruders at Penn—outsiders—and they also thought of the *DP* as belonging to an in-group of which they were not a part. It was not likely that they would brave the imaginary barrier in large numbers without specific and personal efforts to bring them in.

It is also true that nothing appeared on the crisis calendar during my years as president of Penn more often than matters of race and cultural diversity, and I don't think Penn was peculiar in that regard. One of the lessons of the 1960s is that the stresses and strains of the broader society are going to show up more quickly on college campuses than elsewhere. In my more optimistic moments, I consoled myself with the thought that we were having so much trouble because we had been so successful. We had created a very diverse campus community, so we were working on a very tough problem that the broader society had not yet begun to face in a serious way. That is ironic but true.

I remember a conversation I had with a Penn alumnus in San Francisco who I hoped would become a major donor. Finally, he said that he did not want to make a major gift to Penn because he had experienced a lot of anti-Semitism when he was there in the 1930s. Instead, he was thinking about making a gift to Harvard. I wanted to say, but didn't, that the reason he had experienced anti-

Semitism at Penn in the 1930s and not at Harvard was that Penn had admitted him while Harvard had a quota that kept him out. Indeed, one of the things Penn can be proud of is that it never had a Jewish quota, as other elite eastern universities did in the first half of the twentieth century. That is the origin of the strong Jewish presence that is a characteristic of Penn.

Still raw in contemporary Penn memory were the wounds inflicted by the controversial visit of Minister Louis Farrakhan to speak on the Penn campus on April 13, 1988. The visit was the masterwork of Conrad Tillard, an especially dynamic and articulate black student leader, who is now Conrad X, one of Minister Farrakhan's lieutenants in New York. At Penn, he dedicated himself to bringing Minister Farrakhan to campus to speak. The invitation from the Black Student League (BSL) that he engineered was as legitimate as the countless other invitations to outside speakers from Penn organizations that the University accommodates on a regular basis. The BSL had a right to invite him, and the University had an obligation to make it possible for him to be heard. There were several worrisome aspects, however.

One problem was that Farrakhan would attract a large number of people from off-campus: friends, enemies, and the curious. We worried particularly about a confrontation between the Jewish Defense League and the Fruit of Islam. The potential for violence was huge. A bigger problem was presented, however, when we learned that the Nation of Islam, Minister Farrakhan's organization, wanted to dictate the security arrangements, and in particular insisted on searching everyone who came into the auditorium. That required an extended public discussion on campus that I thought was very healthy. An informed and public decision to use metal detectors at the entrances to Irvine Auditorium made it less likely that the devices would spark hostile reaction or chill debate. We eventually worked out an understanding about security that satisfied the Nation of Islam and that also left us in control of the situation.

What was not avoidable was the animosity stimulated between Jewish students and black students. There was much discussion in the *DP*, and there were even meetings between black student leaders and students from Hillel, where the opposition to Farrakhan was being organized. The most disturbing thing to me, as I told the *New York Times* at the time, was that white students "really do have a hard time understanding how deeply offended and angry black students get when they run into racial stereotypes and insensitive remarks on campus. That is what I hear from my students and faculty all the time." That, of course, is why someone like Minister Farrakhan appealed to them.

"At the same time," I said, "I think black students just don't understand why Minister Farrakhan is so incredibly offensive to whites and to Jewish students in particular."[1] The run-up to the speech was tense.

One day Conrad Tillard burst into my office (with a *DP* reporter in tow) and denounced the anti-Farrakhan demonstrators who were out in front of College Hall and elsewhere on campus. He demanded that I have them dispersed. I replied that he would probably not want to be part of a university in which the president had the power to disperse peaceful demonstrators or otherwise to prevent dissent. He stalked out, probably pleased that he had ratcheted up the confrontation a bit.

The day before the event itself, I issued a statement making clear my disapproval of Minister Farrakhan's black nationalism, and especially denouncing his anti-Semitism, but asserting the overriding interest the University had in remaining an open forum for debate and for the expression of ideas.[2] There was no other issue during my tenure as president of Penn on which I got more mail from outraged alumni than the appearance of Louis Farrakhan. "I believe in free speech," ran the logic of the typical letter, "but Farrakhan's brand of hate doesn't merit protection."

On the evening of the speech, I had a regularly scheduled

dinner meeting of the senior officers at my house. We went through our discussions of long-range plans, while across campus a potential disaster impended. We had taken elaborate security precautions, and we had the cooperation and participation of the Philadelphia police, but such events are unpredictable. In conversation with the Jewish student groups, we had reached agreement about how the counter-demonstration was to occur. They wished to minimize the chance for violence, but they also wanted to make their presence and disapproval known. The uncontrollable factors had most to do with off-campus folks, and with things that might happen spontaneously inside the hall.

I remember what a huge relief it was to get the call from the student-life official in charge that night. We were still sitting around the dinner table talking about seemingly safe and distant resource allocations. The report was that the event had gone off with a minimum of problems and that the area around the auditorium was now clear. There had been a huge amount of tension in the auditorium and outside, but there had been no incident that might constitute a violation of University rules. I thanked the community in a public letter the next day, saying that as difficult as the event was in every way, it was the University at its best.

So, yes, we had problems with race relations, and we had them because we had worked hard and very successfully to attract a diverse student body.[3] I admired what the military, the army in particular, had been able to do to include members of racial minorities on a basis of equality. Even there, after years of effort, there are differential rates of advancement for blacks, Latinos, and whites, and there are large disparities in the way the members of those groups perceive their treatment.[4] I also looked enviously at sports teams that were able to function as if race were irrelevant.

The military and athletic teams had an advantage, of course. They both had top-down command structures and a very clear goal that everyone agreed on. Universities, in contrast, are extremely decentralized and consultative in their decision making, and they pursue a multiplicity of goals. There is an old joke that students think the university exists to provide parties, the staff thinks it is an employment agency, the faculty think that they *are* the university and should be left alone to do their research, and the alumni see the university as the sponsor of the football team. Furthermore, the commitment of the university to the maximum amount of individual and intellectual freedom makes it more difficult for it to overcome the patterns of living and thinking that students bring with them from their homes in mostly homogeneous enclaves.

That race relations were in a problematic state was reinforced in my own mind a year before the theft of the newspapers when the campus came close to erupting in reaction to the "not guilty" verdict in the case of the Los Angeles police officers accused of using excessive force while arresting Rodney King, an African American. America had followed the case closely. The videotape of the arrest and of the police beating King was shown countless times on television. The "not guilty" verdict seemed to confirm what many black leaders had been saying for a long time: white America is racist. South Central L.A. exploded in destructive rioting, and violent disruptions flared up in various black communities across the country.

As the news of the verdict spread on the campus that day, feelings of both anger and dismay were palpable immediately. I was not surprised to learn that a city-wide protest meeting had been called for that same evening, to take place at DuBois college house, one of our "living-learning" residences, whose theme was the African American experience, and almost all of whose residents were black. I decided that I should stay home that night, to be available in case anything serious were to happen. The campus security force prepared itself, and faculty monitors from the committee that oversaw the Open Expression Guidelines would be present at the meeting. I got the dreaded call from the campus police about 11 P.M. The speakers had finished, the crowd was restless and angry, and they were going to march to my house.

I went out in front of our house. Lucy, very much against my wishes, went with me. The demonstration, about five hundred strong, swung out of the lawn in front of DuBois and streamed down Walnut Street the fifty yards or so to Eisenlohr. The leaders came through the front gate and up the steps to where Lucy and I were standing. As I looked at the crowd, there were some faces I recognized, and others that appeared to be college students, whether from Penn or elsewhere, but there were also older folks. That was not a good sign. I talked with the leaders and told them that I would be willing to speak to the whole group. We went together out into the middle of Walnut Street, leaving Lucy on the steps. Walnut normally is a busy thoroughfare carrying traffic west out of center city, but the police had wisely blocked the intersection at 38th Street, half a block away, as soon as the demonstration left DuBois for my house, diverting traffic away from the scene. The demonstrators simply sat down in the middle of the street, so it was impassable.

I was scared. Even though I had confronted demonstrations numerous times during my years as a provost and president, I was always frightened when dealing with an angry crowd whose emotions might erupt at any moment. As I pushed my way through the crowd to get to the middle, Mike Carroll, a detective whom I knew on the Penn police force, brushed up against me in his blue jeans and baseball jacket, whispered "I'm here if you need to get out quickly," and then blended into the group right around me. I was really glad to see him, but it also reminded me that I was not in the safest place in the world at the moment. No matter how pacific or even jovial an aroused group seems to be at any one moment, the mood can change in a flash. Unruly individuals intent on trouble, and emboldened by the anonymity of being in a crowd, can quickly ignite a destructive melee. I actually worried much less about my own safety than about setting off a riot. I always tried to appear calm and unworried, and I think I managed that well enough. Speaking in such circumstances is a gamble. It is easy to say the wrong thing and set off a reaction. On the other hand, if one can bring reason to bear on the subject, and make human contact, demonstrators are more likely to keep their wits about them and to behave humanely.

As I started talking, the crowd grew quiet. I said that I understood their frustration and agreed with their sense of outrage at the verdict (which was true). I also spoke of the long way we had come as a society since the 1950s, and how much progress Penn in particular had made. Even though the Rodney King verdict dramatized how much was left to be done, we could be much more effective in fighting racism if we worked together in positive ways rather than lashing out in destructive ways. I promised to meet with Penn student leaders the next day to identify things we could actually do. I was not Demosthenes, but they listened.

After I finished speaking, members of the crowd began to make statements. Soon, a man who was clearly not a student got the floor, or rather the pavement, and unleashed an emotional harangue, the gist of which was that whites had to be dealt with by force because they were evil and they only understood force. My heart began to sink. That was exactly the kind of rabble-rousing that I feared.

Immediately, a young woman whom I recognized as a Penn student spoke up and said, "Wait a minute, there are whites with us here," as indeed there were, perhaps fifteen or twenty percent of the crowd. She then went on to say that her mother was black and her father was white and that she loved them both. If we are going to defeat racism, she said, we could only do it by blacks and whites working together. By the time she got through speaking, I had a lump in my throat, and she carried the crowd with her. There was a moment or two of milling about, and then the leaders decided to march off in the direction of City Hall, twenty-four blocks away. They left, shouting slogans, with the police protecting their flanks and getting the traffic out of the way. No injuries and minimal damage resulted. My meeting with the black student leaders the next day went very well.

In the fall of 1992, there had been a flare-up over a story on the front page of the *DP* about Penn's relationship to the nearby black community in West Philadelphia. The picture accompanying the article was of a pathetically derelict black man holding a wine or whiskey bottle. The caption read, "West Philadelphia," as if he were typical of blacks in West Philadelphia or African Americans in general. I agreed with black students, staff and faculty who thought this was insulting and demeaning in the extreme.

There was also an incident in which a late-night initiation rite by the Onyx Society, a black honorary society, taking place within the residence hall complex known as the Quad, had aroused some angry taunts from bedroom windows and the predictable counter-attack from the Onyx members. Water was poured out the windows onto the students below. Eggs were thrown at the windows. Two Quad residents were disciplined, and the incident became a cause celebre among "movement conservatives" on campus.

Very visible among those movement conservatives at Penn was Greg Pavlik, a bi-weekly columnist for the *DP*. To Pavlik, Newt Gingrich was a wimp, the *National Review* was no better than a liberal rag, and Jack Kemp was a candidate for tar and feathers. All were too accepting of big government. He was especially harsh on minority groups for claiming a privileged moral position because of their status as victims, a popular theme of the right wing in their denunciations of "political correctness." Pavlik agreed in print, for instance, with libertarian polemicist Lew Rockwell, whose incendiary argument was that the numbers of blacks lynched throughout American history were puny by comparison to the numbers of whites murdered each year by blacks. Pavlik described himself as an "old conservative" in the tradition of Edmund Burke, but a neutral observer would have a hard time distinguishing him from a garden variety bigot with a good vocabulary.

In his columns, Pavlik regularly chastised the University for "throwing standards out the window" in the admissions process when it came to members of minority groups, for enforcing politically correct behavior, for engaging in mind control in the guise of campaigns against intolerance. "President Hackney drove the message home in eerily Orwellian tones in a January issue of *Almanac*," Pavlik wrote in a February column. "He (*i.e.*, Hackney) impressed upon the campus that anyone that fails to tow the line of the dominant anti-Western agenda espoused by the University will not escape with 'impunity.'"[5] It would, of course, surprise feminists, leftists, international students, and members of minority groups—not to mention trustees—that the University was pursuing an anti-Western agenda.

About halfway through spring term, 1993, a large delegation of black faculty and staff scheduled an appointment and came to see me. This was the kind of meeting that I hated, a meeting in which grievance upon grievance is voiced, yet few specifics are provided. All are generalities. It struck me also at this particular meeting that there was a certain level of performance-for-each-other involved; it was a rite of *witnessing* for racial solidarity. Still, enough words were said by sensible people whom I knew very well, and whose judgment I respected, for me to take their testimony seriously. I managed at least to avoid that dead-end argument that I had witnessed so often in which well-meaning whites would point out that every slight is not intended as a racial slight, and that most whites go through most days not thinking of race at all, only to hear in response that every black person thinks about race every day because it is the filter through which America sees them, so the anticipation of discrimination is an ever-present reality. Shortly after this meeting, on March 18, I published in the *DP* and in *Almanac*, the faculty and staff journal of record, another letter similar to the one that Pavlik interpreted through his own particular lens. In it, I called upon the Penn community to increase its efforts to build a more inclusive and civil community, and I warned that neither harassment nor discrimination would be tolerated.

I realized that the tide of public opinion had turned against affirmative action. We find ourselves as a society in the worst of all situations: the public is tired of the effort, yet the problem isn't solved. One of the most discouraging developments of the last twenty years is that a steady diet of distorted media images and sound bites about welfare queens and Willie Hortons, frequently manipulated for political advantage, has convinced the public that the problem of equal opportunity has been solved, and that members of minority groups posing as victims are frauds. In the eyes of most whites, serious discrimination no longer exists, so no government action is needed—in fact, would be counterproductive—and the natural processes of democracy and the market, if left unhindered to work their magic, will integrate whites and blacks in a natural and unforced manner.

We know from opinion surveys that substantial majorities of white Americans believe that racial discrimination today is not a big problem. They are aware that discrimination exists, but they believe that the incidence is minor and that it can be overcome easily by individual effort. We also know that significant majorities of African Americans perceive racial discrimination to be a constant and oppressive fact of their daily lives.[6] In itself, this is a dangerous disparity, as if whites and blacks were not living in the same society or were not talking with each other. Consider the immediate reactions to the not-guilty verdict in the O. J. Simpson criminal trial: 70 percent of whites thought it was jury nullification, while 70 percent of blacks thought the verdict was proper. When perceptions of the same event can be so different, what chance does society have to develop the level of social trust needed to allow the public to make collective decisions about common problems?

More important, we know from other studies that significant racial discrimination does exist in housing, jobs, education, banking, the criminal justice system, and the ordinary encounters of daily life.[7] Yet, whites do not perceive these continuing injustices, perhaps because it is not in their interest to do so, but more likely because they continue to harbor negative stereotypes of black Americans.

The occasion for the theft of newspapers was the anticipated appearance of the last column of the academic year from Greg Pavlik. Earlier in the spring, Pavlik had so infuriated some black students that they had gone to the Judicial Inquiry Officer to try to charge Pavlik under Penn's untested racial harassment policy. That policy had been worked out over a long period of time, subjected to much public discussion, and formally debated and approved by the University Council, a representative body of students, staff and faculty. It was an extremely narrowly drawn policy that made racial harassment a disciplinary offense under the Student Judicial Code if three conditions were met: (1) a racial slur were made, (2) in a face-to-face encounter, with (3) the sole intent of inflicting pain.

The events of the spring of 1993 have convinced me that it is a mistake to try to deal with matters of racial incivility through behavioral rules backed by disciplinary mechanisms. It doesn't work, and I regret having supported and promulgated that policy despite the widespread support it had within the Penn community. While this particular policy was unsuccessful, I continue to believe that it is crucial for universities to have explicit standards of behavior, or rules of decorum, that might make mediation or some other sort of moral suasion easier when the peace of the community has been violated. At Penn, it wasn't the rule that failed but the quasi-judicial, adversarial disciplinary process that failed; it was brought to an ineffective halt by the glare of a national spotlight and the determined procedural sabotage of one of the participants.

It is morally reprehensible to maintain that the university has no responsibility to protect its students against the sort of harassment that will make it difficult for the student to succeed academically, to participate fully in the life of the campus community, or indeed to enjoy equal rights to political speech. I doubt that anyone would suggest that a university simply ignore cross-burnings outside the Afro-American Studies office, or swastikas painted on the door of Hillel, or gay-bashing slogans chanted by a crowd outside gatherings of lesbian and gay students. Universities must be intellectually unfettered, but they also must provide an atmosphere in which all their members have a fair chance to reap the benefits of belonging to an academic community. "Hostile environments," the term used in the relevant federal regulations, make it difficult for members of groups vulnerable to scapegoating to benefit from belonging to a learning community.

Indeed, the U.S. Supreme Court's 1999 decision in *Davis v. Monroe County Board of Education* (Georgia) makes clear that schools can be held liable if they fail to act to protect a student from sexual harassment from another student. That case involved a public elementary school but, applying the same reasoning, it may well be not only immoral but also illegal for a university not to take some action to protect its members from the effects of hostile environments. Universities, then, are faced with a troubling dilemma: how can they protect free speech and at the same time protect students from harassing speech. A more accurate way of phrasing it might be, how can a university protect free political speech for everyone, including those who might be silenced by threats or insults?

Consequently, while I have absorbed the painful lesson that rules and formal disciplinary machinery don't work very well, and that they are especially prone to fail when political pressure is heightened, which is just when they are most needed, I can under-stand the argument for a narrowly drawn legal prohibition against hate speech, even though I no longer believe in such policies.

According to Professor Thomas C. Grey of Stanford Univer-sity, one can discern two thrusts in such an argument. First, it might be argued that rules of decorum that limit personal insults actually provide an atmosphere in which real political speech is more free. *Ad hominem* arguments and bitter invective actually inhibit the free exchange of ideas.

Second, given the impossibility of tolerating racial harassment, indeed the positive obligation to prevent "hostile environments," it is better to have a clear and narrowly drawn policy (such as Penn had) rather than to have an unstated and therefore broad, fuzzy, and more easily abused practice.[8] For instance, after a full year of discussion and consultation, my successor, Claire Fagin, promul-gated a new Code of Student Conduct designed to solve the problems of hate speech and free speech revealed in the events of the spring of 1993. What follows is the operative provision of the comprehensive policy, under the rubric of "Responsibilities of Student Citizenship":[9]

> (d) To refrain from conduct towards other students that infringes upon the Rights of Student Citizenship. The University condemns hate speech, epithets, and racial, ethnic, sexual and religious slurs. However, the content of student speech or expres-sion is not by itself a basis for disciplinary action. Student speech may be subject to discipline when it violates applicable laws or University regulations or policies.

Among the Rights of Student Citizenship are the right to freedom of thought and expression, and also the right to be free from discrimination on the basis of race, color, gender, sexual orientation, religion, national or ethnic origin, age, disability, or status as a disabled or Vietnam Era veteran. Given my new-found conviction that hate-speech rules don't work, this seems to me to be about as good as one could hope for. Professor Grey, however, might well point out that it is just the kind of broad and fuzzy policy that is easily abused.

On Professor Grey's side in this argument is the fact that we make distinctions between protected and unprotected speech all the time, in law and in the ordinary course of living. At the most obvious level, we have copyright protections that prevent people from speaking if their speech plagiarizes someone else's words. We also have laws against slander, defamation, and libel. Verbal threats and intimidation are crimes. Pro-life demonstrators in front of abortion clinics have the right to express their opinion, but the courts are having a hard time deciding just when that right begins to interfere with the rights of other citizens to enter and leave the clinic. Does the right to speak, for instance, include getting nose-to-nose with someone trying to enter the clinic and shouting demeaning slogans?

The University of Pennsylvania's sexual harassment policy, which is still in force without a ripple of complaint from free speech purists, declares that, "Our community depends on trust and civility. A willingness to recognize the dignity and worth of each person at the University is essential to our mission . . . . We expect members of our University community to demonstrate a basic generosity of spirit that precludes expressions of bigotry," to which I say "amen."

The policy then defines sexual harassment as "unwanted sexual attention" that is threatening, that interferes with an individual's academic or work performance, or that creates "an intimidating or offensive academic, living, or work environment." Whether such behavior is physical or verbal, it is a violation of the University's standards of conduct, yet no one is protesting against it as a "speech code."

In October 1998, Boston College was shocked when a hate message was sent to minority student leaders by e-mail. The message said that Boston College was for "white men," and that minority students should "go back to where you came from." Students were outraged; a mass meeting called upon the administration to find the author and punish him.[10] In 1999, African American students at Penn State received racist hate messages by e-mail that was traced to unknown senders at Temple University. Officials have vowed to track down the perpetrators and punish them. Neither the ACLU nor the editorial page of the *Wall Street Journal* has leaped to the defense of free speech in those cases.[11]

As John Agresto has pointed out, though he is not in favor of speech codes, there is a perfectly good conservative argument for rules of decorum on college campuses.[12] Ironically, the organization that likes to think of itself as the greatest deliberative body in the world, the United States Senate, has rules of decorum precisely to protect its ability to deliberate. The *New York Times Style Sheet*, and presumably other style sheets used in other news rooms, proscribes usages that would disparage particular groups. This sounds politically correct to me, yet no one accuses the *New York Times* of trampling on free speech. So, when I hear anyone say that speech is sacred and simply ought not to be regulated, I suspect I am in the presence of someone innocent of having dealt with speech issues, or someone more intent on manipulating emotions through the use of slogans than in grappling with reality.

Furthermore, we expect governments and other authorities, such as universities, to regulate the time, place and manner of speech as long as such regulations are reasonable and are neutrally administered. The *Magna Carta* of free speech at Penn is the policy statement known as the "Guidelines on Open Expression," which grew out of the turmoil of political protest on campus in the 1960s. The Guidelines define the rights of speakers balanced against the rights of listeners, other speakers, and those who literally don't want to be bothered; it also prescribes the process through which possible violations of those rights will be identified and adjudicated.

The particular problem that the Guidelines were intended to solve was the problem of the suppression by University authorities of speech in the form of demonstrations and other forms of symbolic behavior. A faculty-student Open Expression Committee oversees the Guidelines and sends monitors to events where speech might be threatened. The Guidelines require that members of the university community who are violating the Guidelines be warned that they are in violation, so that they have a chance to desist. If they don't, then they are formally declared by the monitor to be in violation, and only then can the senior person present in charge of security for the event proceed against the offender or offenders. The system is designed to favor dissent and to limit the authority of the administration. Cumbersome though these rules and procedures may be, they actually work in the Penn setting. They work because they are clear and they are applied in an even-handed way.

All of this is to say that I think the question of hate speech on campus is enormously more complex than the vigilante campaign against political correctness will admit. I am also aware that, in the public square, complexity is a fatal flaw. A clear and powerful slogan is much more likely to win, and winning—rather than illuminating the truth—is the goal of what I once called our "drive-by debates." In that arena, I am undone by my training as a historian, which impels me to try to understand all sides of an issue. I am also defeated by my belief, matured in long years of struggle, that truth is more likely to be found in the contingencies and double-folds of reality than in the assertion of simple principles. I recognize that principles really are simple, but I also know from painful experience that the application of simple principles can be very complicated. So, here I am, cursed with the urge given to me by my great teacher, C. Vann Woodward, to understand the complexities and nuances of human situations, yet certain in the knowledge that recognizing complexity is fatal.

In any case, I found out about the attempt of angry black students to charge Greg Pavlik with a violation of the racial harassment policy from Alan Kors, history professor and frequent critic of mine from the right, who called on March 9, 1993, to say that it was absurd to try to discipline Pavlik for something he wrote in the *DP*. I agreed, so I asked my assistant, Steve Steinberg, to call the associate vice provost for University Life, to whom the judicial inquiry officer (JIO) reported, to find out what was going on. He reported that the JIO would not proceed against Pavlik. I called Kors and told him that Pavlik was not in danger.

What I did not know at the time was that the JIO had already written on March 5 to the black student complainants explaining that the racial harassment policy was specifically designed not to cover things written in the *DP* or spoken on College Green. My inquiry had absolutely nothing to do with the JIO's decision in this matter. She was aware that feelings were running very high in the black campus community, so she was handling each complaint with as much "due process" as possible, without for a minute thinking that the racial harassment policy had been violated. Indeed, a very large network of administrators worked feverishly throughout the spring semester to try to respond creatively to the rising anger among black faculty, staff, and students.

That anger was focused upon the *DP*. In addition to the insulting "West Philadelphia" picture in the fall, the new board of *DP* editors early in the spring term ran a front-page picture of a pair of dancers from Africa Art in Motion who were performing at the Christian Association as a part of Black History Month. The bold-type headline over the photograph read, "WE GOT RHYTHM." Whether or not this play upon a negative stereotype was done intentionally, it was appalling, and it made it easier for black students to believe that the Pavlik column was not simply an innocent effort to represent the full range of student opinion on the editorial page but the true feeling of the *DP* editors. Indeed, some of my advisors who knew the new executive editor, Steven Glass, thought the *DP* was being deliberately provocative.

When the JIO informed Pavlik and the *DP* that she was not pursuing the Racial Harassment charges, she also offered to mediate a conversation between the leadership of the *DP* and representatives of the black community at Penn. Glass, asserting his independence from University authority, refused. That is not hard to understand. Not only might Glass be suspicious of the JIO, but he probably was advised by the *DP* lawyer that he ought to assert his legal rights so as to avoid tacitly recognizing some University authority over the *DP*, which is a separately incorporated entity. It is also true, however, that Glass did not on his own initiate any conversations with the disaffected black students.

The formal complaint against Greg Pavlik therefore never happened, but the bitter feelings of black students toward him lingered. If the student judicial system could not be used to get at Pavlik and the *DP*, black students must have reasoned, they would have to resort to civil disobedience. That is what they did on April 15, 1993.

The operation was well planned, but a few things went wrong. The thieves were noticed at a couple of sites. At the University Museum, suspecting that someone was making off with a priceless treasure, a security official pursued and apprehended the black students and then put them in handcuffs, not a regular practice when dealing with students. At another location, a black male was apprehended by campus police but resisted, and he was struck with a billy club several times in order to subdue him. When I first heard of these events later in the day, the director of security, John Kuprevich, was locked in an acrimonious meeting with black student leaders that lasted more than three hours. Other black students were talking with the vice provost for University Life (VPUL), Kim Morrisson, and charging that the security personnel had overreacted and used excessive force in a way that they would not have done had they been dealing with white students. Emotions were running high and an accurate picture of what had actually happened was impossible to get.

A *DP* reporter called me in the early evening, while confusion still reigned on campus. Off campus, the second Rodney King trial was in the hands of the jury in California. The reporter quoted me correctly in the paper the next day:

> Today's events are only an expression of deeper running feelings on the campus and in society in general, and those more important, deep feelings about the ways in which we relate to each other on campus need to be discussed and resolved by the entire campus community.
>
> We will examine the particular incident today and make sure justice is done, but the bigger issues will remain and we cannot let them fester.
>
> I am saddened that this comes up. I think we were genuinely working at the underlying problems and making some progress, and today's events set us back considerably.

Later, in the evening of April 15, a group of about thirty African American women students came to Eisenlohr, having been meeting all evening among themselves about the events of the day. Several of them came in, and we sat in the living room and talked, though none of us knew just what had happened. They were upset about the reports they had of police brutality, and they recounted the grievances of black students in general. I promised to take their views into consideration as we sorted things out during the coming days. The next day, April 16, the *DP* story on the theft quoted my 1987 policy statement that it is a violation to steal newspapers and that offenders will be held accountable.

There was considerable conversation among faculty leaders, administrative officers, student leaders and security personnel on that Friday. The situation was still tense. The possibility of further disruptions was recognized by everyone. As we talked among ourselves that Friday, and also talked with the *DP* and black faculty and student leaders, members of my staff and the VPUL's staff were acutely aware that the jury verdict in the second Rodney King trial was due to come out at any moment, and we remembered how close the campus had come to riot a year previously in the wake of the first jury verdict. As it happened, the jury announced its verdict over the weekend, finding that the police officers had in fact used excessive force, so justice was delayed but not denied. On that Friday, however, we were fearful of a different outcome.

It was clear to me and others that we had to proceed deliberately, with constant communication among all the affected parties so that no one would be surprised. After a lot of shuttle diplomacy among black faculty and student leaders, student-life personnel, faculty senate leaders, and my staff, we decided and announced that we would create two *ad hoc* groups: an independent commission co-chaired by the provost, Michael Aiken, and the newly arrived executive vice president, Janet Hale, to review standard procedures used by campus police in their dealings with students; and a second group reporting to VPUL Kim Morrisson and Commissioner of Public Safety John Kuprevich that would address the problems existing in the relationship between the police and the minority community on campus. The police didn't trust anyone in the student life area, and the black students didn't trust anyone in the public safety hierarchy. The joint commissions were meant to compensate for that, and also to indicate that we took the complaints seriously. Our assumption was that the incident itself would be handled by the existing disciplinary system.

Over the weekend, my staff and I drafted a statement that

would appear in *Almanac* on Tuesday, April 20, but was released to the *DP* on Sunday so it would have it for its Monday edition. On Sunday, interestingly enough, the *Philadelphia Inquirer* ran an editorial condemning the theft, but on its op-ed page printed two pieces to help explain the "flap": an excerpt from a Greg Pavlik column, and excerpts from a letter previously printed in the *DP* accusing the *DP* of fomenting bigotry on campus and signed by 202 African American students and faculty. The Sunday *Inquirer* also quoted me correctly in their news story saying that the theft had been a violation of the University's Open Expression Guidelines, and that the individuals responsible would be held accountable.

The *DP* on Monday was full of material on the newspaper theft, of course. "Members of the Black Community" were reported to have issued a statement asserting that they had simply been exercising their First Amendment rights. The head of the Philadelphia Fraternal Order of Police was quoted extensively defending the behavior of the police. A statement of The Working Committee of Concerned Black and Latino Students, issued to the *Washington Post* over the weekend, was quoted also, accusing the police of using excessive force.

It bothered me that the *DP* article based on my statement badly mischaracterized it, and that the *DP* chose not to print the entire statement so readers could interpret it for themselves. The article reported correctly that I had defended the right of the *DP* to publish, but then it went on to say, "Hackney—noting that 'two important University values, diversity and open expression, seem to be in conflict'—stopped short of condemning the theft." It is hard to know what words would have counted as "condemnation." I had made it clear that the superior claim in this conflict was free speech and a free press, and I had stated publicly that the thieves had broken University regulations, but those things apparently were not enough.

More troubling was the statement from Steven Glass, the executive editor: "On the basis of numerous tips that the newspapers would be stolen again, the *DP* has asked the University to comply with its agreement to provide unfettered distribution of the newspaper. The University has rejected this request." That was a very dramatic and damning announcement. It established, of course, a heroic plot line that was eventually taken up and followed by the mainstream press: a young, twentieth-century John Peter Zenger stands up for press freedom against a craven university, a university surrendering to the moral and physical extortion of black students, a university corrupted by political correctness. What a story! The problem was that it was totally fabricated. Steven Glass had not talked to me or to anyone in the administration.

Elsewhere in the same Monday paper, Vice President John Gould was correctly quoted as saying, "The University recognizes the right of the *DP* to distribute its papers. The University will follow all of its procedures and use all of its resources to protect that right." John Kuprevich, the head of campus security, was quoted as saying virtually the same thing.

In retrospect, the Steven Glass fiction, as well as the story line it was meant to promote, makes more sense to me. When he graduated in 1994, Steven Glass was helped by Alan Kors to get a position at the conservative Heritage Foundation, whence he launched his journalistic career. In 1998, Glass, by then a rising star reporter for *The New Republic,* was exposed as having completely invented a number of stories that had appeared in *The New Republic* over an extended period of time. We have no way of knowing why he resorted to wholesale fabrication, nor do we know when he began the practice on a grand scale, but we see him in this little vignette during his editorship of the *DP* ignoring the demarcation between truth and fiction in order to set up the narrative he wished this story to follow. He had the help later of others in the real world of big-time journalism, for whom inexperience could not be an excuse, but they also had a strong ideological interest in this same story line. Together, they were remarkably successful.

He was so successful, in fact, that I became irritated about his continued misrepresentation of the facts, and especially of his misrepresentation of my position. I have no way of knowing how many off-campus reporters talked to Glass in order to get some orientation to campus events. Such consultation would have been a natural thing for any interested journalist. I do recall getting so frustrated by the continued reports in the mainstream press that I had not condemned the theft of the newspapers that my staff drew up a fact sheet of quotations in which I declared the theft to have been wrong and a violation of University policy. Against the advice of Penn's general counsel, I also sent a letter to the *DP*'s lawyer on June 14 setting forth my efforts and statements since April 15 to make it clear that I disapproved of the theft of newspapers. "I am more than a little annoyed that your client, the *Daily Pennsylvanian*, continues to spread untruths about me and the University. I keep hoping that the canon of journalistic ethics will come into play at some point, or at least some ordinary intellectual honesty. I will keep hoping."

On the day following the *DP*'s confusing coverage, Tuesday, April 20, my statement was printed in full in the *Almanac*. As I have admitted in public several times since, I wish that I had written the statement in a way that did not permit misrepresentation. On the other hand, it is clear that I was deliberately misunderstood and misrepresented because it was in the interest of the *DP* that everyone understand the issue as being about a free press, and *only* about a free press. If it was *also* about racial insensitivity on campus, then the *DP* was cast in a more negative light, and the story doesn't work as well for them.

As is so often the case these days, this was a struggle to define the meaning of the event, to frame the issue for the public in a way that would insure that one's political position prevailed. Given this reality, and the needs of the occasion, I am not sure that I could have made my statement tamper-proof. I needed to make clear that the theft of newspapers was unacceptable behavior, and that open expression was the primary value of the University. Yet, for reasons of intellectual honesty, and to avoid inflaming an already tense situation, I could not fail to acknowledge in some way the grievances of black students. I confess that I also hoped—perhaps a forlorn hope—to preserve something of my dream of a harmonious and diverse campus community. The operative two paragraphs of my statement were as follows:

As I indicated above, two important University values now stand in conflict. There can be no compromise regarding the First Amendment right of an independent publication to express whatever views it chooses. At the same time, there can be no ignoring the pain that expression may cause. I deeply regret that these recent events may mask the continuing effort the University is making towards a comfortable and permanent minority presence in a diverse and civil University community. Whatever the consequences in the weeks ahead, the University will continue to work diligently and persistently towards both goals.

As individual members of an academic community who grasp the importance of both of these values, we must work together to narrow the distance that now seems to preclude their peaceful coexistence. Neither is dispensable, and both are central to the character of the Penn community. We cannot afford to continue to pose them as incompatible alternatives. Penn must be both a diverse and welcoming community for all its members and one in which freedom of expression is the supreme common value. As a free forum for ideas, the University must be open to all and open to all ideas or it is not free.

Elsewhere on the same page of the *Almanac*, I placed another statement:

> Though I understand that those involved in last week's protest against the *DP* may have thought they were exercising their own rights of free expression, I want to make it clear that neither I nor the University of Pennsylvania condone the confiscation of issues of the *Daily Pennsylvanian*. I want to remind all members of the University community of the policy I promulgated several years ago (*Almanac* 7/18/89, reprinted below) specifically banning such actions. Any violations of this policy will be pursued through the University judicial system as chartered by the schools of the University.—Sheldon Hackney, President

On a separate page of the same edition of the *Almanac*, there was another statement by me, entitled "Reflections on the Second Rodney King Verdict." In it, I say, "Neither I nor the University can condone the infringement of the rights of a free press or the suppression of any individual's right of free speech." Anyone then or later interested in knowing my position on the theft of the newspapers could not fail to learn it in unequivocal detail from the most public, widely circulated, official, and unimpeachable source.

David Hildebrand, the chair of the faculty senate, also placed a helpful statement in the *Almanac*: "Penn didn't look very good last Thursday. The confiscation of most copies of the *Daily Pennsylvanian*, and the subsequent altercations involving police and security personnel, should trouble all of us. Copies of the *DP* have been seized before. The seizure was wrong, then and now. In a university, we cannot, must not, will not suppress ideas, however odious. 'I'm all for free speech, but . . .' just won't do. I have a request for all involved: Please get down off your high horse. If we all adopt postures of injured self-righteousness, we will only aggravate the tensions revealed by this incident, to no useful end. The standard response to these tensions is 'We must talk to each other.' Perhaps, but even more, we must listen to each other. Too much of our talk is a dialogue of the deliberately deaf. To use our skills and our understanding, we need to hear the positions and concerns of others. Dare I suggest that we listen to the other folks before framing our response? Might help."

That was the last week of publication of the *DP* for the academic year, but the newspaper theft case kept boiling along in the off-campus press. By the time Reunion Weekend arrived, it was still on the minds of the *DP*. Steven Glass and three *DP* reporters interviewed me for the reunion edition, May 14. In the transcript as printed by the *DP*, one can detect a little badgering from the interviewers and a little testiness from the interviewee:

DP: Regarding the theft of the *DP*s, why didn't you just come out and condemn the action?

Hackney: I've been over this—if I were the *DP*, I certainly would be doing what you're doing right now, which is saying that event meant nothing else than a violation of the open expression guidelines. They were certainly a violation of the open expression guidelines and I think I indicated that in the first document I wrote in the midst of the crisis and I indicated it again very clearly—maybe not as stridently as you would have wanted—in the second that I wrote over the weekend. But the event also had other dimensions to it that I did not want the community to lose. The event was not a protest against the open expression guidelines, it was a protest against the *DP*; the allegations were that the *DP* was racist and insensitive. Now whether you agree with it or don't agree with it, the fact that a significant proportion of our community felt strongly about that is something the community ought to face and ought to talk about. And I didn't want that to be lost.

DP: Couldn't you have said, "Yes, there are these major

concerns that are important and we need to make sure everyone feels comfortable at Penn. However—"

Hackney: That's exactly what I said—

The question to ponder is how and why my words and actions were reinterpreted even as they were being reported to the public. Given the subsequent portrayal of me as having equivocated on the question of whether the theft of the *DP* was a violation of University rules, and as having defended the perpetrators rather than prosecuting them, the clarity of the *Almanac* notices above suggests a malevolent kind of instant revisionism at work. As George Orwell put it most cynically, "Who controls the past controls the future. Who controls the present controls the past." Who controlled the telling of this story to the public?

3

Buffaloed At Penn

O N April 26, 1993, the *Wall Street Journal* carried an unsigned editorial under the headline, "Buffaloed at Penn." This was the first mention in a mass circulation journal of the obscure disciplinary case that had been fumbling its way through Penn's student judicial process all spring. It had not even been mentioned in the *DP* on campus. The *WSJ* not only brought the case to national attention, aided by its reliable chorus of true-believing conservatives (Rush Limbaugh, George Will, Charles Krauthammer, Cal Thomas, and John Leo), but the *WSJ* editorial page also defined the terms in which the incident was to be understood. There was a major avalanche of media attention, but almost everyone followed the script written by the *WSJ* editorial page.

The incident in question happened on the night of January 13, 1993, at the very outset of the spring term. A group of black women students was celebrating their sorority's Founders' Day. They were singing and dancing loudly outside a high-rise residence hall on Penn's campus. White students in the dormitory began shouting out the window at the celebrating women below. What began perhaps as a jocular exchange turned ugly. Insulting words were hurled back and forth, including sexual and racial slurs of the most crude sort. This was, after all, only a couple of months after the notorious Onyx Society incident in the Quad, and it developed in much the same way. The black women became especially infuriated when they heard themselves taunted as "nigger bitches." They went for the campus police. By the time the police arrived, the white students in the dorm had melted away. As the police inquired among students on the floors that had been engaged in the affair, the only student who admitted to participating was Eden Jacobowitz, a freshman who had spent much of his childhood in Israel.

Jacobowitz told the police that he had yelled, "Shut up, you water buffalo. If you want to have a party, there is a zoo over there," referring evidently to the Philadelphia Zoo, which is only about a mile north of the campus. The women thought they heard him refer to them as "black water buffalo." The confrontation was an ugly event that the University could not ignore, but it should have been handled by Penn informally through mediation, bringing the involved parties together so they might learn from each other why tempers had flared up, and why the words that had been used had stung so much. That some sort of mediation was not used is the result of (1) the atmosphere of racial tension at the time, (2) the specific anger of the black women about being insulted, and (3) the tempting availability of the racial harassment policy, with punitive sanctions attached.

The judicial inquiry officer (JIO), the "prosecutor" in Penn's then existing disciplinary system, investigated the case, talking to everyone involved, though no additional students were ever identified. She attempted to reach some settlement with Jacobowitz, who was willing to apologize, but who was not willing to have any notation made on his record. The aggrieved women were not willing to let the matter drop. After a bafflingly long period of time, the JIO brought formal charges against Jacobowitz on behalf of six complainants. This happened on March 22, two weeks after I had inquired about Pavlik, and four days after I had published my letter to the campus community on diversity and civility, but three weeks before the White House announced the President's intention to nominate me for the NEH chairmanship. At some point during the spring term, Jacobowitz secured Professor Alan Kors as his advisor. The Judicial Charter permitted accused students to be represented by another member of the Penn community, but not by outside lawyers.

My relationship with Alan Kors has been a curious one. As a zealous libertarian, with a tilt toward conservatism, and with remarkable rhetorical gifts, Kors was a visible commentator on campus affairs, always ready to give a *DP* reporter a sound bite designed for the headline. He is also an excellent teacher, which redeems a lot of sin in my scheme of values. On many things we agreed, including the importance of free speech in general and academic freedom in particular.

On some things we differed. For instance, I think that romantic relationships between faculty members and students are wrong. No matter who initiates them, nor whether they are consensual, faculty members of whatever gender or age have an obligation to avoid them as long as the object of their desire is a student. Faculty-student relations are particularly unethical when the student is under the supervision of the faculty member in any way, but even without that kind of direct conflict of interest, the trust that should exist between students in an institution and the faculty of that institution is undermined by sexual entanglements. Suspicions of favoritism, fears of exploitation, and a general degradation of authority will inevitably result from these relationships. The important mission of the institution will be subverted. Kors, on the other hand, thinks that what transpires among consenting adults is their own business. Kors was therefore a loud critic of my policy against faculty-student liaisons.

Throughout the spring of 1993, Kors complained vigorously of the "kangaroo court" provided by the student judicial procedures because they were closed to the public. I thought then, and still think, that students who are accused of wrongdoing ought not to be exposed to public judgment and condemnation. Not only should the disciplinary process be humane, but it should be treated as part of the educational process. There is, in addition, the federal law forbidding universities from disclosing personal information about their students. Kors also had been a vocal critic of the racial harassment policy and of the diversity education program administered by the vice provost for University Life.

Lurking in these policy disputes is a clash between different conceptions of what the university is. I do not think Penn is simply another street corner or public park where strangers can harangue each other, nor is it a retail store for instruction where sellers meet buyers by appointment to conduct transactions that involve only glancing relationships. It is not a collection of autonomous individuals who have no obligations toward each other. It is a community in the real sense, a community with a particularly important purpose. Members of such an educational community are related to each other through an intricate web of obligations and privileges, depending upon each person's role in the educational mission.

More heretically, I see students as not yet completely adult. I would like them to have a great deal of independence, and I think a part of the mission of a residential university is to encourage self-discipline and self-reliance, and to guide students toward the time when they must take full responsibility for themselves. In my view, the campus should be a somewhat sheltered environment within which students can test themselves and even experiment with various possible answers to the question, "Who am I; what sort of person do I want to be?" It should be a more forgiving and a more nurturing environment than is society at large. Over the years, for instance, colleges have assumed police power within their own jurisdiction so that the disciplinary environment might complement the instructional mission of the institution. I much prefer having campus police and deans and faculty watching over students than, say, the Philadelphia police with their limited repertory of arrest, jail, and criminal court.

Alan Kors speaks for those who see college students, even those of traditional college age on a residential campus, as fully adult.[1] That sounds wonderful. It is a completion of the 1960s revolution in student power that made *in loco parentis* politically incorrect. There are, however, grave implications. In particular, it diminishes the university's ability to shape the residential and co-curricular environment in ways that contribute to the education of the student, and it leaves the student extremely vulnerable to exploitation by more powerful adults in the community, not to mention running afoul of civil authorities in a way that could have dire long-term consequences.

Despite our differences, Alan Kors and I maintained a cordial relationship. When Kors was picked by Lynne Cheney to be a member of the National Council on the Humanities, I provided a laudatory evaluation during his pre-confirmation investigation. I do not regret this; he was an excellent member of the Council. When my name surfaced in the press in February as a possible nominee to be chair of NEH, I got a very flattering letter from Kors urging me to pursue the job and assuring me that I would not find the NEH to be a "hornets nest of ideologues or ideological agendas."

"On the critical matters of curriculum and scholarship," Kors wrote, "I have admired, very deeply, your commitment to an open and pluralistic university, both with reference to substance and with reference to procedure. In the midst of the storms, you have secured the proper mechanisms of due process, peer-review and a commitment to an open-minded and diverse educational university. I believe there is universal recognition of your integrity and fairness that would serve the NEH ideally."[2]

Circumstances change, of course. In an exchange between us in the *DP* in the wake of the publication of his book in 1998, a book in which I am elevated to the lofty position of emblematic villain, Kors trashes my presidency with hyperbole almost as astounding as the claim of his book that "universities have become the enemy of a free society":[3] "Hackney writes of 'shared governance' at Penn," exclaimed Kors. "Having both centralized power and destroyed that shared governance, infantalizing students and marginalizing the faculty, he lacks the moral authority to utter those words."[4] For some reason, I never felt quite that way.

I first learned of the Water Buffalo episode from Kors when he called me, probably soon after March 22, 1993, when Jacobowitz had been formally charged by the JIO. I told him in that first call that I knew nothing about the case but that I would find out and call him back. I again asked Steve Steinberg to get the facts. Later, Steinberg reminded me that when I had spoken at Hillel on the first Friday evening of the term, Jacobowitz had been there, as had Steinberg. A group of students had gathered around me chatting and, according to Steinberg, Jacobowitz had described his predicament, insisting that he was not guilty of racial harassment. I apparently was sympathetic and told him that he should go through the process, tell the truth, and he would be OK. I still do not remember this, but I have no reason to doubt it.

I had been badly burned earlier in my Penn career when a group of fraternity members had shown up on my doorstep late at night complaining that they were being pursued by the JIO for sexual misconduct. I gave them the same sort of advice, but I apparently sounded too sympathetic. They told a lot of people the next day, including the JIO, that I had agreed that they were not guilty of anything. It turned out, as one might expect, that they had not told me the whole story. The facts of the case were damning. I was subjected to scathing criticism by women's groups and sympathetic others not only for taking sides but for taking the wrong side.

As it worked out, in a very painful and protracted process, the offending students were exonerated after a hearing before the most respected senior faculty member of the Law School. I nevertheless was thenceforward always careful not to appear to take sides or to short-circuit due process.

When Steinberg reported back to me in March 1993, he gave me the facts of the incident very much as I have related them above, and he also brought the news that the formal charges had been served and the judicial process had been set in motion. Unlike the Pavlik situation, the assistant JIO had decided to proceed. I called Kors back, told him what I knew, and said that I could not intervene. *It is crucial to understand that the Penn system was set up specifically to exclude the president and provost.* With regard to disciplinary cases, I was similar to a mayor, who cannot tell the district attorney what to do, and I was not at all like the chief executive officer of a corporation, who can tell anyone in the organization what to do. That a college president does not have the power of an army general is a bit of "context" that my journalistic stalkers neglected to pass along to their readers.

Part of the reasoning for setting the judicial process up to be independent of the president and provost was to avoid using the time of those two officers in disciplinary cases. Part of the reasoning was also to mimic the American legal system by making the judicial process as impervious to outside pressure as possible. This was a reasonable worry. If the daughter of a wealthy donor were in trouble, or if the *WSJ* were bashing the University, or if the chairman of the appropriations committee in the state legislature were asking that the son of an important constituent get favored treatment, the temptations would be great. Who knows what grubby political, public relations, and pecuniary motives might warp the delivery of justice if the president and provost were involved? Still, as I will make clear later, the Penn system was not good. The president and the provost need to have the ability to get involved earlier in cases of alleged student and faculty misconduct, if necessary. They are going to be held responsible, so they should have some means of intervening in extraordinary circumstances.

Kors called me several times in the next few weeks, always demanding that I simply order the JIO to drop the case. I always declined. It struck me as ironic that one so punctilious as Kors was about the principle of due process was pressuring me to throw due process out the window. Kors was also calling other people in my office and in the VPUL's office. On April 7, I got a long memorandum from Steve Steinberg describing an hour of conversation on the phone with Kors arguing for intervention on several grounds, including the ground that the JIO was making a mockery of my public statements about the intent of the racial harassment policy, as well as the argument that Penn students should not have less free speech than society at large. He ended by saying that if we were set on not intervening he would stop the phone calls and pursue the defense of his client in other ways.

Shortly thereafter, Eden Jacobowitz hand-delivered to my office a copy of his long, eloquent, contrite letter to the JIO that argued again that the term "water buffalo" had no racial meaning and that he, Eden, had had no intention of hurting the women complainants. Furthermore, the letter charged that the JIO was sending his case to a hearing panel simply because the JIO did not want to take personal responsibility for ruling that the charges of the women did not amount to a violation of the racial harassment policy. Jacobowitz was probably right about this. Even though the JIO—actually, the assistant JIO, who was handling the case—had the authority to decide whether or not there was enough merit to the allegations to warrant sending them to a faculty-student panel, given the fact that the JIO was herself black, and was a relatively junior administrator, the pressures would have been enormous.

I sent a copy of the Jacobowitz letter to Steve Steinberg on April 12 with a handwritten note: "If this guy gets convicted it will be a horrible miscarriage of justice, but I suppose there is nothing to do but let the process play out and hope for the best from the Panel. You ought to alert Carol Farnsworth [our press officer] that we may be getting some negative attention from the NAS (National Association of Scholars, a group in which Kors was active that had been organized to resist the radicalization of universities)."

In his follow-up memorandum to all the people within the administration who dealt with the press, the public, the trustees and the alumni, Steve also mentioned that we could expect to hear from Accuracy in Academe, the Anti-Defamation League, and the American Jewish Committee. Steve also pointed out that Jacobowitz's letter had indicated that copies of it had been sent to powerful presumed allies outside the University: Harvey Silverglate, prominent ACLU attorney and later the coauthor with Alan Kors of a book that prominently included a discussion of the Water Buffalo case; Alan Dershowitz, law professor at Harvard; Nat Hentoff, columnist for the *Village Voice*; Dorothy Rabinowitz, member of the editorial board of the *Wall Street Journal*; and George F. Will, nationally syndicated columnist. The posse was being formed, and their telephone reconnaissance calls began almost immediately.

Linda Hyatt, my chief-of-staff, sent me a quick note also on April 12 describing an agitated telephone conversation she had with Alan Kors. He was "revved up pretty high," she reported. "Alan brought Jesse Helms, national spotlight, the whole nine yards into it." She asked me to call Alan and try to convince him again that letting the disciplinary process be completed was the best course of action. I tried. At the end of that long and tortured conversation, Alan said that if I didn't end the Jacobowitz case, "I will have to go public." I knew exactly what he meant.

By the time of that letter from Jacobowitz, and the last round of telephone conversations, President Clinton's intention to nominate me was public knowledge, making me an attractive target, and the demonization of Lani Guinier was visibly underway, demonstrating what I could expect from a politicized process. Therefore, all of my personal political interests lay on the side of getting rid of these cases as fast as possible. As the threatened political campaign exploded in the news media, and the strobe light of negative publicity flickered incessantly, trustees began urging me to find some way to end the agony, and even my colleagues among the senior officers were pressing me to get the University out of the headlines. My staff and I spent agonized hours worrying the question of whether or not I could intervene.

Nevertheless, I could not see a rationale that was either "constitutional" under the University's rules of governance, or fair to the five black women who had a right under University policy to have their complaint adjudicated by a faculty/student panel. In addition, to have intervened simply because Penn was suffering from bad press would open the University to extortion by publicity. To have intervened also would have thrown the University into a crisis both racial and constitutional. By the time those crises made themselves felt, I would have been safely installed in Washington, but I could not bring myself to use Penn in that way.

On April 17, the Saturday after the theft of the newspapers on Thursday, I sent an e-mail message to the ten people who were nursing the dual crises with me: "Thanks for the news about the Kors contingent circling for the kill on the Water Buffalo case. Getting everyone together is a good idea. At this point, I still think all we can do is let the judicial process work. We can't lose our courage when facing to the right any more than when we are facing to the left."

Penn was subjected to such a drubbing in the press that anyone doing a retrospective evaluation is tempted to conclude that any alternative course of action would have been better. That is because the pain of what happened is clear, but the consequences of alternative courses of action are difficult to imagine. Those consequences of my intervention would not have been as public, perhaps, but they would have been more serious and longer lasting. Members of minority communities at Penn would have been outraged by additional evidence that the University put a lower value on their interests than on the interests of other constituencies, even to the extent of being willing to violate the University's own policies and procedures. The University would have been extremely vulnerable to legal suit. Faculty, staff, and students who care about "constitutional" due process and "shared governance" would have been offended. Just because we have not heard from the people who would have been angered by my intervention does not mean that they were not there.

Over the course of my career, I have discovered several rules of university political behavior. One fits here. In any controversial situation, once the decision maker has acted, the winners shut up and the losers raise hell. In fact, the winners not only shut up, they hunker down out of the line of fire and try to pretend to their friends and colleagues who are raising hell that they (the winners) are totally sympathetic to the losers and had nothing at all to do with the decision that the losers are protesting against. The decision maker thus is a political vagrant; he has no visible means of support.

Because Kors had been straightforward with me, I was not surprised by the *WSJ* editorial when it appeared on April 26. It was not until later that I learned that the *Forward*, the former Yiddish language daily, whose editor was a former editor at the *WSJ*, and who was also a friend of a friend of Kors,[5] had published a story on April 23 under the title, "Pennsylvania Preparing To Buffalo A Yeshiva Boy," leaving little doubt that readers were meant to understand the story in the context of black-Jewish tensions. The *WSJ* loosed its campaign three days later, on the day scheduled for the Jacobowitz hearing.

The first two sentences of the editorial make its purpose clear:

"A freshman, the latest victim of the ideological fever known as political correctness, goes on trial at the University of Pennsylvania today. It's not irrelevant to note that the head of this institution, Sheldon Hackney, is President Clinton's nominee to head the National Endowment for the Humanities and a man, university spokesmen insist, committed to free speech." Thus, the story is positioned as evidence in the running conservative critique of liberalism and liberalism's habitat on college campuses, and conservatism's determination to delegitimize President Clinton at the outset of his term in office.

The incident itself is described by the *WSJ* as "Kafkaesque" and an example of the "theater of the absurd." Jacobowitz appears as guileless, willing to cooperate with the police, truthful, and innocent of any harmful intent. He is dutifully studying when he is rudely disturbed. The reader pictures him passively looking out the window and gently requesting that the noisemakers be more quiet so he can work. In contrast, University authorities are presented as aggressive, determined, out of control, intimidating toward white students, and illogical.

More important, in the mental picture that became the template for almost all subsequent accounts, the women do not exist as individuals.[6] The reader never sees them as real people. In fact, they scarcely exist. Similarly, the other white students drop out of the account. The reader envisions Jacobowitz as being alone and not as part of a group, and certainly not as part of an ugly, intimidating, and raucous mob. This literary treatment does not falsify any fact, but it shapes and colors the story by what it leaves out, what it de-emphasizes, what adjectives and adverbs it chooses, and what context or lack of context it provides. Try to imagine this story being "successful" if Jacobowitz had been firmly positioned as part of an unruly mob hurling racial slurs at vulnerable black women, women who had names and whose individual stories were known to the reader in the same way that Jacobowitz's was.

For instance, notice what happened to John Rocker, the star pitcher for the Atlanta Braves in 1999, when he made crude and demeaning statements about gays, immigrants, and a black teammate in an interview published by *Sports Illustrated*. Not only did media and public disapproval descend upon him, but the Commissioner of Baseball fined him $20,000, suspended him for a period of time, and required him to attend "sensitivity training." Even though the players' union sprang to his defense, the public didn't seem to think his right to free speech was violated. The difference between Roker and Jacobowitz is that Rocker's words were unambiguous, whereas Jacobowitz's words were ambiguous at worst and his story was told in a way that presented him in the best light. Change the narrative, even without falsifying any of the facts, and the meaning also changes.

It is interesting also that this first *WSJ* editorial argues the case for Jacobowitz being innocent of racial harassment, rather than arguing against racial harassment policies in general. Penn's problem in the eyes of the *WSJ* editorial page, at least at the outset, was not that it had a rule against racial harassment but that Jacobowitz had not broken it. Professor Dan Ben-David of Penn is cited as suggesting that "water buffalo" had popped into Jacobowitz's mind because it is a literal translation of the Hebrew word, "behameh," which is used as a mild pejorative, akin to the English slang term "dumb ox." Two black Penn professors are quoted as denying that "water buffalo" had any history as a racial slur in America.

All of this is fair enough, but it simply ignores the long history of animalistic representations of African Americans as part of white supremacy's mind game, and that is specifically the sin that John Rocker committed when he called a black teammate a "fat monkey." It also ignores the question of what the women thought they heard and why they got so angry. This is an example perhaps of a cultural disconnect, of the same words carrying different significance in different cultures. It was a "teachable moment" that was squandered by Penn and also by the mainstream press.[7] It was also a moment that was hijacked for ideological purposes.

The hearing that was to have been held on April 26 was postponed by the judicial administrative officer (JAO), a retired professor of medicine, whose task it was to make the machinery of justice work. I did not envy him the job of dealing with Alan Kors, who has a knack for lifting the most mundane matter to the level of fundamental principle in the blink of an eye, and then the tenacity to worry the matter until everyone involved is so exasperated that they are willing to do whatever is necessary to get an agreement and move on. On this occasion, the JAO had made the decision to postpone the case until the fall semester because the faculty advisor to the complainants had decided to withdraw and they did not yet have another advisor. Postponement was unfair to Jacobowitz, of course, because he would have to live even longer with uncertainty. It was also unfair to the women, some of whom were graduating and would not be around the following year. The end of the term was rapidly approaching, so the JAO had a serious problem, and so did the University. A second *WSJ* editorial crucified Penn for the muddled postponement.

My thinking at that time is revealed in a memorandum that I sent on April 28 to Linda Hyatt, my alter ego on everything:

> On the assumption that you will be going to the meeting Mike Aiken [the provost then and now the chancellor of the University of Illinois, Champaign-Urbana] is pulling together tomorrow on the Water Buffalo case before you and I see each other, let me pass on an additional thought. Someone suggested today that a number of the closely implicated parties were noticing that they were losing the public relations war on racial harassment and so were thinking of changing the charge to simple violation of the behavior code. Initially that sounded okay to me

because it got the racial harassment policy out of the way. On second thought, however, I think it is a bad idea even if someone has a right to do it. Jacobowitz has been accused of racial harassment and I assume this has not made him happy nor made it easy for him to concentrate on his exams, etc. While his advisor may be responsible for it, his name is also plastered all over the country as having been accused of racial harassment. To change the charge now both denies him the right to clear his name and will seem to the world that the evil University discovered it couldn't get him by direct methods so it is going to get him by indirect methods. There is also the problem that he was probably not noisier than other students who were yelling out the window, and indeed he was probably not noisier than the women students they were all yelling at. I think that tack has serious problems.

If there is a way to get the hearing done this semester, that would be good. If those who are bringing the charges reconsider and decide that there are insufficient grounds, that is even better. Of course, we have to worry about the rights of the complainants who feel aggrieved (at this point in my conversation with the fanatic editorial writer for the *Wall Street Journal*, she snarled, "is that all it takes? One black student feels aggrieved and someone is guilty?"). In any case, it should be an important meeting.

My conversation with the *WSJ* referred to above came about when Carol Farnsworth, director of the Penn office of press relations, told me that the *WSJ* was preparing to run a third editorial. Carol thought that I ought to call to see if I could dissuade them, though she was not optimistic about that. I therefore called Dorothy Rabinowitz, the member of the editorial board who had written the first two editorials and who was clearly camped on the case.

To her I explained the situation as I saw it. The charge of violating the racial harassment policy had been made. We had a prescribed process through which the case would be adjudicated, and I was obligated to let that process work. I did not have the power to intervene in the case, nor was I permitted to discuss the substance of the case, I told her, but I was confidant that, if the case were heard by a faculty-student panel, justice would be done. Though I did not say this to her, I felt certain that no faculty-student panel would punish Jacobowitz.

I asked Ms. Rabinowitz not to write another editorial until the campus process had run its course. There was a pause. Then she said in a voice so chilling that I knew immediately that, like Dr. Seuss's Grinch, she had garlic in her soul, "This is the darkest moment for human freedom in the history of Western civilization, and you, sir, are complicit."

I was stunned. Given my sheltered existence, I was not as aware as I should have been that the editorial page of the *WSJ* was messianically ideological. This was a brutal way to pick up that little piece of information. I was also amazed at the sweep of her accusation. Had she not heard of the Creel Committee during World War I, or the Red Scare afterward, the internment of Japanese Americans during World War II, or McCarthyism, or the FBI's counter-intelligence campaign against the radicals of the 1960s, or Richard Nixon's dirty tricks during the election of 1972? To my admittedly biased mind, Penn was pretty small stuff in the great sweep of Western civilization. Where does the Inquisition fit, anyway?

I remember asking her in shock if she were really a journalist. There was no immediate answer to that rhetorical question, so I hung up. That was rude. I am glad my mother does not know I behaved that way. She would not have approved.

The long *WSJ* editorial appeared on May 10. It began by singing the praises of yet another in a long line of intellectual vigilante groups on the right,[8] the American Academy For Liberal Education, whose purpose was to restore liberal education to what it had been in the mythical past, "before the legions of the politically orthodox succeeded in converting so many institutions of learning into ideological re-training centers." The appearance of this organization, the *WSJ* wrote, "is especially heartening in light of what is going on at the University of Pennsylvania."

The editorial then provides *WSJ* readers with Ms. Rabinowitz's version of our conversation. According to her, I insisted that the prescribed disciplinary procedures had to be followed because the sorority women felt aggrieved. "Did the complainants' mere feeling of grievance justify the administration's punitive campaign against a student—for using a term clearly having no relation to a racial slur? Yes, Mr. Hackney told us, the women's feeling of grievance required redress." Ms. Rabinowitz had apparently been listening only with her right ear.

She went on to quote with approval the statement of a member of the board of the Massachusetts chapter of the American Civil Liberties Union that "the Penn administration is one of the most cowardly and craven of any major university." I particularly hated being *both* cowardly *and* craven. Nevertheless, this became the standard judgment from which few dissented. "The craven Hackney," the *St. Petersburg Times* editorialized on May 19, "who soon will be going to Washington to head the National Endowment for the Arts [sic], a federal pinata for the nation's artists, responded to this assault on a free press with mush. . . . Unfortunately, on the issue of free speech, Hackney is a wimp."

Usually, in the abbreviated accounts of newspapers, the Water Buffalo case and the theft of newspapers are conjoined. I am described as responding to the theft of the newspapers only by saying that "two important university values—diversity and open expression—seem to be in conflict." Readers were left to think that I was trapped somewhere in that closed feedback loop, unable to make up my mind. Countless times that spring, news accounts described my response in just that simplified and incorrect way, a truncated version of the truth that was promoted by the *WSJ*. In the public image being created of me, it was not exactly clear whether I was a left-wing drill sergeant or a dithering nincompoop.

Before its campaign was over, the *WSJ* editorial board had not only colored the reports of the events at Penn in ways that were not flattering to me, they also published a number of outright untruths: that I had failed to say that the theft of the newspapers was wrong; that I had defended the newspaper thieves on the ground that they were exercising their right to free speech; that I had punished a Wharton professor for insulting black students in class; that I had proposed banning ROTC from the campus because of the anti-gay policies of the military; that I defended political correctness on the grounds that it promoted a free exchange of ideas; that I defended blasphemous slogans written in chalk on Locust Walk in support of a visit by the controversial artist, Andres Serrano; that I followed a double standard in protecting controversial left-wing speakers but not people on the right. All of those charges were demonstrably wrong.

Imagine my surprise, then, when I learned much later that Alan Kors had complained to the chairman of the board of trustees, Al Shoemaker, about a summary of facts about the events on campus in the spring of 1993 that went on July 23, 1993, to alumni covered by a letter from Jack Reardon, who was then the president of the Alumni Association. It is not surprising that Kors found the summary at odds with his version of events. It is revealing, however, that he finds no fault with the *WSJ*. "The University simply is telling lies," Kors wrote to the chairman, "and the WSJ has said nothing deceptive at all." The chairman replied that the summary seemed reasonable to him.[9]

My mother-in-law, Virginia Durr, was staying with us that spring while these events were transpiring. She is an early riser, while I prefer to start the day more slowly and with as little conversation as possible. I had learned over the years how with minimal effort to hold up my end of a conversation over breakfast with her about whether the contradictions of capitalism were at last about to bring it down, how McCarthyism was poised for another attack on freedom, and whether racism is the result of the repressed psycho-sexual rape complex of Southern white men, and other such light breakfast table topics. Even though I did not agree with her general understanding of how the world worked, we had a wonderful relationship. I had long since forgiven her for writing her friend, Jessica Mitford, during Lucy's and my courtship, "Lucy's new beau is a right nice boy but will never amount to much."[10]

I remember coming downstairs one morning in late April thoroughly dejected by the caricature of me that was filling the newspapers. I was still on the stairway, a room and a half away from the kitchen where Virginia was having her coffee and reading the paper, when I heard her excited voice calling out, "Sheldon! Come here! You won't believe what they are saying about you this morning."

Virginia was totally loyal, though. Without my knowing it, she was calling everyone she knew in the world of journalism and pleading my case. When I finally did get to Washington and met Paul Duke at a party, the long-time moderator of the PBS program, "Washington Week in Review," said, "Oh, yes, you must be the guy Virginia Durr was calling me about." He was not sympathetic.

Meanwhile, newspapers, magazines, news broadcasts, and talk shows all over the country were filled with stories about an appealing young student being persecuted by Penn's thought police because of a crazy interpretation of innocent words. Eden Jacobowitz became a folk hero for the conservative cause. He made a very sympathetic guest on television and radio talk shows.

I was astounded when I learned of the postponement of the hearing. This was the worst possible situation for everyone concerned—the University, me, the women, Jacobowitz. The provost and I and the vice provost for University Life urged the JAO to schedule another hearing so the matter could be resolved. To his credit, he saw immediately that it had been a mistake to postpone the April 26 hearing, but the University was now in the midst of the exam period. He scheduled a hearing, therefore, for May 14, a week after the end of exams, the Friday of Reunion Weekend, just before Commencement the following Monday. This was the last possible moment.

Even though he and his advisee had been eager to dispose of the matter earlier, Kors now got the JAO to agree that the hearing on May 14 would not be dispositive. It would only hear Kors's argument on his procedural motion to drop the charges. The JAO agreed that the hearing would not go into the question of guilt or innocence. I have no idea what he was thinking about, but I do know how hard it is to resist the relentless pressure of Alan Kors when he is in full cry.

To make matters worse, the JAO did not tell the other parties to the hearing that he had done this deal with Kors. They all arrived expecting to go through a regular hearing. The result was that no one was happy. Penn again looked inept, if not malevolent. The panel, frustrated by their inability to complete the hearing, warned Kors not to comment in public, and they announced that they would give their procedural report to the VPUL within ten days.

To the delight of the huddled masses of reporters waiting outside the hearing room, Kors emerged with a handkerchief clenched between his teeth, indicating that he had been gagged. As he revealed later, as soon as he was out of the public eye that night, he immediately gave his version of the hearing to Dorothy Rabinowitz at the *WSJ*.[11] The result of this was another round of exclamation-point headlines and full-throated denunciations. For me, there was more standing in the public stock. Worse, it meant that when the First Lady came on that Monday to be the Commencement speaker, she would be walking into a national spotlight with the press listening to every nuance of her words to determine what she thought of the Water Buffalo incident. I felt very badly about that.

I normally love Commencement. Everyone is in a good mood. It is the last exercise of the academic year, and it is not only celebratory but it portends a change of pace in my life and in the annual cycle of the University's life. Penn's Commencement ceremony is held in Franklin Field, a location that exudes tradition and even a little splendor. About twenty-five thousand people are in attendance, family and friends of the four thousand or so undergraduate, graduate, and professional school students who are about to receive their degrees. The energy level is sky high. Candidates for degrees form-up in "Hamilton Village," the campus region of residence halls and open lawns just west of 38th Street. The academic procession moves east on Locust Walk, the major pedestrian spine of the campus, passes between the parted ranks of faculty, trustees, and honorary degree recipients in front of College Hall, and then winds its way to the stadium entrance on 33rd Street. It is colorful and joyous.

Lucy went to the airport to meet Hillary and ride back to the campus with her. I waited in the lobby of the Annenberg Center which serves as the robing room for trustees, faculty and the platform party. When the First Lady arrived, a buzz went through the crowded room. After some instruction from the marshal of the procession, we fell into ranks and walked out of the Annenberg Center, across its broad plaza and then down Locust Walk a hundred yards to take our places in front of the statue of our founder, Benjamin Franklin, sitting benevolently between the library and College Hall. As the giddy students passed by us, they slowed to wave or call to the First Lady; some ran over to stand by her for a photograph snapped by a friend. The First Lady generated more reactions from the procession as it went by than had Bill Cosby a few years earlier, but then he had not had a new haircut. I noticed that as Hillary stood there smiling and responding to the students going by, she was also talking to Katie Couric who had slipped into place beside the First Lady with a microphone.

Observing all this good feeling and happiness, I nevertheless felt very tense and very tired. I was worried about any sort of unpleasant display of opinion because there were an unusual number of reporters and television cameras poised to pounce on the least little thing. Penn students sometimes become quite playful and irreverent on these occasions, building elaborate model structures on top of their mortarboards, passing beach balls over their heads from one side of the assembly to the other, blowing bubbles, raising good-natured signs asking for jobs, doing the wave at solemn moments, and similar youthful indiscretions. In addition, such high-profile events are ideal for anyone supporting a cause. About fifty Jacobowitz sympathizers, with their mouths taped shut in sarcastic response to the disciplinary panel's admonition against speaking in public about the case, had demonstrated outside my house only two weeks before. On Saturday, as I had walked around among the reunion tents on campus talking to alumni, I encountered a number of people wearing "Free Jacobowitz" buttons. Some sort of display was clearly possible, but I was hoping it would stop short of being disruptive or disrespectful.

The surprises began to appear fairly early in the fast-paced program. When I finished my remarks, in which I touched upon the American identity and the problem of multiculturalism in a post-Cold War world, themes to which I returned many times in succeeding years, the graduating seniors stood and applauded with warmth. I was touched. I interpreted this to be not necessarily an expression of agreement with me on the controversies of the spring but of approval of my performance in the presidency over twelve and a half years, despite the roiling mess that I had just gotten the University into.

Then, after Provost Michael Aiken had announced the honors won by various students, and the incoming chair of the faculty senate, Barbara Lowery, had made her remarks, I got up from my seat at the rear of the platform to go forward to the microphone to announce the honorary degrees. I lost the race to the microphone to the chairman of the trustees, Al Shoemaker. I thought he had lost his place in the script, if not his mind. Then he announced, "Will Lucy Hackney come forward?"

My wife appeared in academic gown from the side of the platform where she had been led by my assistant and our friend, Linda Hyatt, who was in on the surprise, as Lucy and I were not. Al then proceeded to read the citation and to bestow a much-deserved honorary degree on Lucy, the juvenile lawyer, founder of Pennsylvania Partnerships for Children, member of the board of the Children's Defense Fund, and energetic conjurer of community on the Penn campus. There was loud and approving applause. It was a wonderful thing for the trustees to have done. In addition, while I was deprived of the microphone, Al also awarded an honorary degree to me, an act of affirmation that meant a great deal to me under the circumstances.

The First Lady handled the delicate situation beautifully when she spoke. She began by making a joke about her new haircut, which indeed was not only the talk of Locust Walk during the procession, but the fixation of the press afterward. "When the President called for sacrifice and asked everybody at the White House to give him a 25 percent cut, I decided to go for a 50 percent cut to do my part."

She clearly had to comment upon the Penn controversies, and she did so deftly.

She spent a long paragraph describing the nation's challenge: to find ways to celebrate diversity without fracturing our communities. "We must always uphold the idea of our colleges as incubators of ideas and havens for free speech and free thought. And our country and our colleges must also be communities . . . where every person's human dignity is respected. Freedom and respect are not values that should be in conflict. But we cannot debate our differences nor face our mutual challenges unless and until we respect each other, men and women, young and old, across the ethnic and racial lines that divide us. I know that you share . . . the general distress that any acts of hate, hateful acts, hateful words, hateful incidents that occur too frequently today in our communities and even on our college campuses." About this time in her talk, I was contemplating a charge of plagiarism.

Later in the address, she said, "We must be careful not to cross the line between *censuring* behavior that we consider unacceptable and *censoring*. . . . For all the injustices in our past and our present we have to believe that in the free exchange of ideas justice will prevail over injustice, tolerance over intolerance and progress over reaction."[12] This, of course, is the line that was quoted most frequently in the press the next day. Led by the *Philadelphia Inquirer*, the press generally interpreted the First Lady's remarks as being a rebuke to me. "Finally, someone got it right at Penn," the approving *Inquirer* editorial stated, praising the First Lady for not condoning the theft of the campus newspaper, "an act that departing president Sheldon Hackney initially described as a seemingly acceptable 'protest.'" The *Inquirer* editorial board apparently trusted the *WSJ*'s editorials more than the *Inquirer*'s own reporting. The *Inquirer* had reported on the Sunday after the thefts, April 18, that I had "said individuals responsible for confiscating the student newspaper on Thursday had violated the university's open expression guidelines and would be held accountable." As the *Inquirer*'s factual error on May 18 had appeared first in a *WSJ* editorial, it strikes me as clear evidence of the extent to which the *WSJ* editorial page was driving the story. Lest the reader think that I have fallen prey to paranoia, the *Inquirer* later simply reprinted the *WSJ* editorial of June 9, thus saving themselves the trouble of translating it into their own prose.

It is also a measure of how the "story" had taken on a life of its own, so that "facts" were adjusted to fit the needs of the story.

Though I never said the theft of the newspapers was an acceptable protest—that was an argument made by the perpetrators and their outside lawyers—the story works much better if I am seen as being on their side. I am, then, more clearly the personification of political correctness. I also believe it is possible that the *Inquirer* editorial board did not consciously lie when they claimed that I had defended the theft as a legitimate protest. Once they decided that the story was about "political correctness run amok," then the facts of the case began to fall into place, whether those facts existed or not. The story line begins to create the "facts," rather than the other way around.

The *Inquirer* front-page reporting of Commencement is also instructive. The lead, of course, is that Hillary Clinton defended free speech. Then the story accurately describes the enthusiastic student response to Hillary Clinton both on Locust Walk and then in the stadium during her talk. She used themes that were familiar for her, the reporter noted, "but she clearly tailored her remarks on freedom and obligations to Penn's recent controversies." Nothing wrong so far. The problem comes because the reporter must tell the reader what those recent controversies are:

> Two incidents in particular have drawn extraordinary attention.
>
> In one case, a black student group seized one day's press run of the *Daily Pennsylvanian*, the student newspaper, in protest over perceived racism. In the other, Penn's judicial system brought racial harassment charges against a white student who called a group of black women "water buffalo."
>
> In both cases, Hackney and other top administrators have been widely criticized—with many commentators saying that Penn has been too mild in defending principles of free speech, and too quick to comply with groups on campus who would curb speech they view as racist.

The problem here is not that this summation contains erroneous information, but that it functions merely to perpetuate the
existing "story," a story shaped at the outset to support the conservative political agenda. Notice how the reporter slips from the
active to the passive voice, thus avoiding responsibility for the truth
or falsity of the criticisms while also evading the task of providing
an account of specific transgressions that the reader might use to
judge the merits of the controversy for himself. I am, then, guilty of
having been criticized, indeed for having been criticized by un-
named people with unexamined motives. Like celebrities who are
famous for being famous, I am controversial because I have been
criticized—and vice versa.

"Hooray for Hillary," the *St. Petersburg Times* trumpeted. "In
her commencement address at the University of Pennsylvania this
week, Hillary Rodham Clinton spoke words that desperately
needed to be heard by students, faculty and especially by Sheldon
Hackney, the university president."[13] I was Robert Novak's "outrage of the week" on "Capital Gang."

For my part, I felt less chastised than envious of her rhetorical
dexterity. In any case, I was delighted because she had not been
embarrassed in any way, and she had taken advantage of the
situation to make an excellent impression both locally and nationally. She seemed genuinely pleased with the day. For Penn, it was
terrific.

That night on "Crossfire," Michael Kinsley introduced the
topic of free speech on college campuses by describing the situation
at Penn and also the case of Leonard Jeffries, who had just been
removed as departmental chair at City University of New York
because of his anti-Semitic and anti-white comments. Kinsley then
quoted Hillary Clinton's earlier paragraph in her Penn address,
which sounded very much like my formulation of the problem: we
need to protect free speech and avoid hate speech at the same time.

"Pretty hard to argue with that, eh, Pat?" he said. His ideological opposite number, Pat Buchanan, did not take the bait. Instead, he made fun of the notion of punishing someone for calling other people "water buffalo" and failing to punish the black students who had stolen the newspapers. "Isn't that a rather vicious double standard?" he asked.

Ruth Sidel, psychology professor at Hunter College, then gave a response that was so simple and so reasonable that it apparently was overlooked by almost all of the mainstream press that spring while the Penn story was still hot. She pointed out that the University was merely saying that the matter of whether "water buffalo" is a racial slur should be determined in the regular way by a faculty-student disciplinary panel, and that the perpetrators of the newspaper theft also should be pursued through the regular University disciplinary procedures.

Later in the program an even more remarkable thing occurred. Michael Kinsley was questioning Dinesh D'Souza, the *enfant terrible* of the conservative movement, and asked why a university should not be able to set disciplinary standards for its students. In particular, he said, a university cannot have students running around calling black students "niggers" and calling other students similar epithets. D'Souza agreed with that principle, and so did Pat Buchanan! Kinsley and Buchanan ended the program agreeing that universities could not simply allow students to call each other hateful names, but that Jacobowitz should get off without punishment because his offense was petty, and the students who stole the papers should be punished. Those are conclusions with which I agreed. I am indebted to Kinsley and Professor Sidel, even though their clarity on the subject did not change the way that mainstream journalists continued to report the events.[14]

The day after Commencement, I began the ticklish business of mediating a solution to the Water Buffalo case, following the approach that I had outlined to Steve Steinberg by memorandum on May 15, the Saturday of Reunion Weekend:

> As you might imagine, I have been thinking of little else but our current dilemma, in between talks and glancing conversations with several thousand alumni. I come to the same conclusion you do. To her credit, Linda (Hyatt) was there several days ago. I don't see anything to do now but to stick by our principles and let our student disciplinary process run its course, even if that is a September hearing. There are real problems with that, but I would not feel very good about aborting the process unless there were some extraordinary event that screwed it up very badly again. I do believe that we ought to see if we can't continue to get the message to the complainants that it is not too late for them to seize the high road in this by withdrawing their charges and stating their case in public, after explaining that no one was benefiting from the current situation. That is a long shot but worth a try. Otherwise, we try to steer a straight and steady course.
>
> Thanks for worrying with me.

So, I communicated with the advisors of both sides, and my message was the same: no one is benefiting from the situation. After a tense week of discussions among themselves and with their advisors, the women decided that they would drop their charges against Jacobowitz. They had come to the conclusion that they would never get their side of the story out until the case was ended and they could speak publicly. As they were working their way to that disagreeable position, I was afraid that Alan Kors would make another grandstand play that would sour the atmosphere and freeze things in place. He returned my call late one night when I was already asleep at Don and Ann Brown's house in Washington, where I had spent the day trying to round up support for my nomination. I explained to him what the situation was, and he promised me that he would keep silent and would not initiate any legal action while these conversations were proceeding. He kept that promise.

At the press conference on May 24, the students announced their decision to drop the charges. They made it clear that they were upset that they had been required to remain silent while they were ridiculed in the press, and that they felt thoroughly abused because their side of the story had not been told. With regard to the incident itself, they said they had heard Jacobowitz call them not just water buffalo but "black" water buffalo. Moreover, his shouts were part of a general barrage of insults, including "the N word" and the "word for a female dog." Of course, they were offended. Professor Peggy Sanday, their advisor, Professor Houston Baker, and Trustee Gloria Chisum had all been extremely helpful to the students as they thought their situation through. In addition, those three appeared at the press conference and spoke sympathetically about the plight of the complainants, bound as they had been to silence.

No effects of this effort were discernible in the press reports about the news conference or later. National Public Radio did an honest and complete job of reporting, and what the Associated Press put on the wire was as accurate and balanced as one could expect in five hundred words. However, more typical of what actually appeared in newspapers was the sixty-six word coverage of the *Christian Science Monitor*: "Five black women called "water buffalo" by a fellow University of Pennsylvania student dropped their racial-harassment claim on May 24, complaining that the accused man had turned the news media against them. The case against Eden Jacobowitz had been seen as a case of political correctness run amok and an embarrassment for university president Sheldon Hackney, President Clinton's choice to head the National Endowment for the Humanities."[15]

The *WSJ* editorialized on May 25 that the case "revealed what the descent of America's campuses into the mire of speech codes and harassment codes has wrought. What they have wrought, namely, is an assault on free expression and reason that is virtually without precedent in a modern, free society." I wondered about what the *WSJ* thought of the death squads in Guatemala, Pinochet in Chile, the dirty war in Argentina, apartheid in South Africa and similar situations, but it would have been churlish to raise those questions.

In her syndicated column, Ellen Goodman, as usual, arrived at a wise judgment about the case. No one at Penn is happy about the outcome or the case, she observed. The easy lessons are about politics. Jacobowitz became a "prize show horse." "Penn became a whipping dog for conservatives because they were after bigger game: the outgoing president, Sheldon Hackney. . . . But the harder lessons are about the university as a microcosm of society." America is struggling with issues of diversity, she pointed out. In the broader society, the law is the chief tool for conflict resolution, but "if the only tool you have is a hammer, everything starts to look like a nail. . . . The law creates winners and losers, not cohabitants." In short, the problem in both society and at a university is trying to deal with a real problem with the blunt instrument of an overly legalistic system instead of with talk aimed at increasing understanding.[16]

In the fall, with the events of the previous spring safely put to rest, and with me out of the way, Provost Marvin Lazerson appointed a board of inquiry to find out what had gone wrong with the judicial process the previous spring. Jacob Abel, former chair of the faculty senate, and one of the most respected members of the faculty, was the chair. The board issued its report in April 1994. The provost welcomed their report because, he said, it described how the judicial process had failed when it had become politicized. The report also concluded that Jacobowitz had not been treated fairly, but the five young women had been treated even worse and had suffered more harm. The JAO was criticized for allowing Alan

Kors to manipulate the process on behalf of Jacobowitz. The board also made some sensible recommendations: the process needed to be speedier; mediation should be used more; and there should be a group (note: not the president or the provost) that supervises the bringing of serious charges by the JIO.

Displaying his knack for deft understatement, Alan Kors said, "The farce continues, and the members of the committee should be ashamed of themselves."[17]

In addition to my function as a cudgel with which conservatives could batter President Clinton, and as the anti-hero of the running narrative that conservatives had created that was designed to undermine the moral authority of liberalism, there is an additional large lesson to be learned from the journalistic treatment of the two events of the spring. Those who shaped the public perception of them were not trying to inform the public so much as to capture its attention. Leaving aside the extent to which the *WSJ* and a small group of conservative commentators consciously molded the story to fit their ideological purposes, one must still explain why mainstream reporting merely amplified the version of events being constructed by the *WSJ*. Part of it is certainly that the theft of the newspapers struck journalists right in their self-interest, but there is more to it than that.

When the mainstream press first learned of the Water Buffalo story, they learned it from the *WSJ* editorial page. The story line was already set. In addition, the Water Buffalo story was easy to shape into a story of an innocent individual oppressed by a cruel bureacracy. It had an appealing victim, Eden Jacobowitz, who was tested but eventually triumphed over a bullying university. It needed an identifiable villain, all the more satisfying if he were powerful and privileged, and much better if he were a person rather than a group or an abstract idea. I was available for that role. For the story to work well, there could be few ambiguities or contradictions, few bothersome realities that would get in the way of the plot. It had to be stark. For instance, the counter claims of the black women students on the sympathies of the public must be muted. The hero had to be protected from any suspicion that he was engaging in unattractive mob activity. Procedural due process had to be portrayed as obfuscation and inhumane bureacracy. Their strategy worked beautifully.

The infamous April 20, 1993, edition of the *Almanac* also contained my letter of resignation as president, to take effect no later than June 30. Al Shoemaker and I had concluded, as soon as the President's intention to nominate me had been announced on April 9, that my fate was not likely to be decided for weeks, if not months, and that the University needed to know who was going to be president in 1993-94. It was therefore better for the University for me to step down right away and unconditionally, so an acting president could be named and could be fully in place when the new fiscal year started on July 1. I had already named the interim provost, Marvin Lazerson, and he was beginning to take over from Mike Aiken. As soon as Claire Fagin, dean of the Nursing School, had been selected as the interim president, I began consulting with her about any decision that would play out during her term. That included the disposition of the newspaper theft case.

The Open Expression Committee on April 27, in response to a request from the vice provost for University Life, issued its advisory opinion, declaring that the incident of April 15 had been a violation of the Guidelines on Open Expression. The VPUL appointed Professor Howard Arnold, from the School of Social Work, a highly respected member of the faculty who is black, to serve as a special judicial inquiry officer for the case. On September 13, long after I had left office, he submitted his report. He found that the students in question had violated university regulations, but because of a number of factors, including the absence of any effective effort on the part of the University during the 1992-93 year to respond in an educationally appropriate way to the festering complaints of the black students, as well as the campus community's need for healing, he resolved that he would not seek to punish the perpetrators and that the matter was closed.[18]

In receiving Professor Arnold's report, President Fagin and Provost Lazerson amplified his reasoning. After assuring the community that no future violations of the policy against confiscation would be tolerated, they wrote:

> As an educational community, however, the University has a special responsibility to see that conflicts between students are not only resolved, but also that they are used to educate us all about the difficulties of living in a diverse society. The University must be a place where students can learn from their inevitable mistakes and misjudgments. That is essential to the process of education. Therefore, our aim is to get everyone involved in this case to work together and to learn from these painful experiences through constructive communication. We and they must put this matter behind us and get on with the educational mission of the University.

4

It's Not About Me

I N THE MIDST of the delicate negotiations with the parties to the Water Buffalo case, on Friday, May 21, 1993, I had a telephone conversation with Arlen Specter that was a serious blow to my chances of confirmation. He was as mad as he could be that I had not come to see him earlier. My story had been in the newspapers since mid-April, yet I had not come to see the senior Senator from my home state. He was deeply offended. I apologized. I groveled, if one can do that on the telephone. I then tried to explain the timing of my approach to him. Perhaps he had noticed that there had been serious business on the campus? Consequently, I had just begun to turn my attention to Washington. He was not mollified. My heart sank. He abruptly ended the conversation by saying, "Talk to my AA [administrative assistant] and we'll take it from there."

The press conference ending the Water Buffalo case was on Monday, May 24. While I was holding my breath during that event, Specter's office called to set a time for me to meet the following day with Barry Caldwell, the administrative assistant. On Tuesday morning, Lucy drove north, headed for the Vineyard, our refuge. In low spirits, I took the train south into the fiery furnace. Nestor Davidson, my "sherpa" (in Washington slang), from the White House Office of Legislative Affairs, met me at Union Station and guided me up to the "Hill," to the Senate Office Building and Specter's office. I thought that we might as well have been scaling Everest itself.

Nestor was only two years out of Harvard and looked even younger. I found him intelligent, energetic, savvy, and completely compatible, but I was beginning to be a little nervous about the course of events and the advice I was getting. No one among the half dozen folks in the White House with whom I had conferred about the confirmation process had mentioned that it would be a good idea for me to go see Senator Specter. Arlen acted as if I had violated one of the most sacred rituals in Washington, but when I mentioned this to my supporters in the White House, they shrugged as if it were news to them. I was clearly traversing dangerous terrain whose warning signs were not only unknown to me but apparently to my guides as well.

Nestor sat through my meeting with Barry Caldwell, who turned out to be very pleasant, responsive, and straightforward. He was a Dartmouth alumnus, but I restrained my usual urge to engage in male Ivy League banter. I thought the meeting went well. We also heard later that the Senator had tried to get back in time for the meeting, so perhaps a thaw was in progress. On the other hand, if one believed in *realpolitik*, one would expect Arlen to withhold his support until he was sure I could be confirmed and/or until he could get something in return.

Prospects for my confirmation were not bright. The *WSJ* attacked again at a critical moment: "Mr. Hackney and friends have spent considerable time in recent weeks complaining that 'conservatives' have distorted his views and that he roundly condemned the taking of the papers. What Mr. Hackney in fact did after the theft was to issue a statement awash in pious evenhandedness, which repeatedly exculpated the seizure of the papers as 'a protest activity.'"[1] That, of course, was not an argument that I ever came even close to making; it is a complete fabrication. Several years later when Dorothy Rabinowitz, the author of all the *WSJ* editorials about me, won a Pulitzer prize for a different editorial campaign, I found myself wondering if the Pulitzer jury worked like the college newspaper competition, in which truth is not a factor.

The *Washington Times* gave a preview of what I could expect from it if I ever got to Washington. It ran an article by Tom Knott dripping with sarcastic derision of Penn for the Water Buffalo case. I was dubbed "Mr. Wimp" for the occasion:

> To think, Mr. Wimp previously was a big defender of free speech. He didn't have a problem when Robert Mapplethorpe's explicit photographs were shown on campus. What's wrong with a bullwhip sticking out of some guy's backside? Why, its educational, is what it is. And when Louis . . . Farrakhan spoke on campus in 1989, Mr. Wimp thought it was stimulating. But Mr. Wimp has been inert over the water buffalo issue. Last week, he said, "Our university . . . is experiencing some very painful conflict. Those problems must be resolved but cannot be resolved here [at the Commencement exercises]." How touching. Perhaps Mr. Wimp has been stuck in his ivy [sic] tower too long. Or maybe his is just a case of poison ivy. . . . And deep thinkers in the college community such as Mr. Wimp wonder why they are such easy targets. Mr. Wimp is not merely guilty of mishandling the episode. Worse, he's guilty of failing to teach Penn's students everyday coping skills.[2]

A search of the Nexis on-line database of journalism for June 9, 1993, returned 486 articles on the subject "Sheldon Hackney," and few were positive. *Time* magazine on June 14 ran a major story under a large picture of me looking worried. It was entitled ominously, "The Next Lani Guinier?"

On the boisterous televised Washington free-for-all called The McLaughlin Group, May 21, John McLaughlin predicted that Lani Guinier's nomination would be withdrawn, as it soon was. Fred Barnes chimed in, "John, you were right about Lani Guinier. She's gone. And there's only a 50-50 chance that Sheldon Hackney, the president of the University of Pennsylvania, will be confirmed as the head of the National Endowment for the Humanities." McLaughlin asked, "Because of the water buffalo scandal?" Barnes responded, "Among others." Others?

The *Republican Faxwire* on June 3 answered that question and informed the faithful about me and the significance of my nomination:

> Hackney has made news by his pusillanimous handling of a racism charge against a Penn student who called two black women "water buffalos." Earlier, he did nothing when black groups seized thousands of copies of the university newspaper because they did not like a columnist that appeared in it. Hackney, a supposed defender of free speech, has said that political correctness is good because, whether the charges are justified or not, they encourage "debate." Rep. Tom DeLay has denounced Hackney's "double standard," and Senate Republicans are considering making a major stink about the choice. In 1991, a Senate committee rejected the nomination of Carol Iannone to an Endowment board because of pressure from feminist groups. It's payback time.

Here, in brief, was the case against me. It was built of partisan interpretations ("pusillanimous handling"), willful misrepresentations ("he did nothing"), outright fabrications ("political correctness is good"), and woefully erroneous history ("double standard"). Furthermore, the theme of "payback time" for the defeat of the Carol Iannone nomination to the National Council on the Humanities was stated with sobering clarity. I was in trouble.

Our Vineyard neighbors and friends, Wendy and Bill Luers, suggested that I consult their friend, Tim Wirth, who had just left the Senate and had written a candid—some said too candid—*New York Times Magazine* article on the state of politics in Washington. He was now parked in the State Department working on global environmental issues. They arranged an appointment for me and briefed Wirth on my need for guidance.

At the appointed day and hour, I showed up, not knowing what to expect. Tim motioned me to a seat next to his desk and began. "I am going to tell you all about the mechanics and the etiquette of Senate confirmation procedures, what to do and what not to do, but first I want to say something very important to you. If you forget everything else I am going to tell you about how to get confirmed, this is the one thing that you must not forget—it is not about you." I must have looked a little surprised because he went on to explain in words something like the following:

"It is not about you. There are 535 dramas being acted out on the Hill all the time, and none of them is about you. You may wander into one of those spotlights now and then and be incorporated into one of the dramas, but you will not be the hero. In fact, you will play the part that has been assigned you by one or more of those 535 main characters. You will be made to fulfill the narrative needs of the moment in the career of that Senator or that Representative. So, whatever happens, you have to keep telling yourself that it is not about you; it has nothing to do with the real you."

I have now forgotten all of the procedural advice that I got from Tim Wirth, as good as it was, but I have not forgotten that bit of wisdom. It kept me going during my darkest moments. Then, after four tumultuous but successful years at the NEH, when I was leaving and was therefore making my last appearances before our appropriating committees, I was delighted to hear friends and even former critics heaping praise upon me for saving the Endowment, for de-politicizing it, for guiding it through a reorganization required by a 36 percent budget cut, for working out a new relationship between NEH and the state humanities councils, and for conducting a "National Conversation on American Pluralism and Identity," saying very nice things about me in public from the raised platforms in the hearing rooms. As I was feeling my pride blossoming, Tim's voice whispered in the deep recesses of my mind, "Remember, it is not about you."

Armed with a new attitude, I began the hard work of paying courtesy calls on the members of the Senate Committee on Labor and Human Resources, of which Ted Kennedy was the chair and Nancy Kassebaum was the ranking minority member. Al Shoemaker and Carl Kaysen of the Penn Board were enlisting the aid of trustees who might be close to strategically placed Senators. John Huntsman, for instance, was active in Republican politics in Utah, and Orrin Hatch was an important member of the Committee. Arlen Specter seemed very important because my fate might be decided by moderate Republicans, so Claire Fagin, already designated to succeed me at Penn on July 1, went with David Morse, Penn's director of Federal Relations, to see the Senator and urge him to support me. Lee Annenberg, who had been Chief of Protocol in President Reagan's White House, went to Washington herself and called on Strom Thurmond, who was a member of the Committee. In short, we went on the offensive.

I spent a long weekend on the Vineyard in late May, reading NEH materials and organizing the end-of-year trustee meeting at Penn that was to occur June 17 and 18. It would be my farewell. On May 28, Lucy and I had dinner at the home of Kibby and Tess Bramhall, who were part of our old and close circle of friends. Mary and Mike Wallace, also part of our crowd, who live near us in Vineyard Haven, rode with us "up island" to the Bramhall house in Seven Gates Farm. Along the way, I explained my confirmation difficulties to the Wallaces, who had been following things in the press, especially the *WSJ*. Mike was very understanding and supportive. What amazed him was that the image of me being presented in the press was so much at odds with the person he knew.

Being misrepresented was something Mike understood from personal experience. A few years before, I had prevailed upon Mike to come to Penn to receive an honorary degree and to be the Commencement speaker. Sometime that spring, Mike was in a studio doing an interview. Thinking that the cameras were off, and trying to provoke his subject into lowering his guard, Mike used words that played upon racial and ethnic stereotypes in a way that critics immediately labeled as racist. A huge controversy ensued. On campus, the United Minorities Council, led by the Black Student League, demanded that Mike be disinvited. The story was played up in the *DP*. A major embarrassment was in the works.

Mike and I talked about the situation. I could not blame him for walking away from a possible confrontation at Penn, but he didn't want to do that. So, I talked to the black student leaders and told them that they were wrong about Mike Wallace. They weren't convinced by me. Mike could also have taken the position that he was coming to speak and security was my problem. He didn't do that either; he offered to come down and meet with his critics. They agreed to talk to him. Without any publicity, they met in my office in College Hall for several hours one afternoon. I left them together and went somewhere else. When the black student leaders came out of that long conversation, they unanimously said they would be proud to have him as their Commencement speaker. They made their support public and vocal. That conversation was, indeed, a conversion. Mike gave a wonderful Commencement address; it was even more of a triumph than most of the audience could appreciate.

In 1993, in a characteristic act of courage and friendship, Mike volunteered to write Orrin Hatch on my behalf and to write a letter to the editor of the *WSJ*. He did not have to take on my fight, to associate himself with me in the depths of my demonization, but he did so. His letter appeared on June 17 and undoubtedly had an effect. He argued simply that the caricature of me that was being bashed in the press was not at all the individual that he had come to know over a long number of years.

For his trouble, Mike drew a rejoinder from the *WSJ*: "A note from CBS's Mike Wallace, published in our letters column last week, chides us for judging Mr. Hackney by his mistakes and adds: 'he has inevitably fumbled. Who hasn't?' We were deeply moved by Mr. Wallace's solicitousness on behalf of those who make mistakes, and wait with interest to see whether his concern for fairness might one day be extended to the public figures mercilessly flayed and garroted on '60 Minutes' every week."[3]

Tom Ehrlich, who shared my foxhole at Penn for five years and was now president of Indiana University, wrote a supportive letter-to-the-editor of the *Los Angeles Times* on June 22. I also got an unsolicited boost from Bob O'Neil, former president of the University of Virginia who was still in Charlottesville teaching law and directing the Thomas Jefferson Center for the Protection of Free Expression. Responding to a column by George Will, Bob wrote in a letter-to-the-editor of the *Washington Post* on June 25 that he did not like racial harassment policies but that to reduce my extensive career to that one incident was folly in the extreme. He argued that I had long been a stalwart defender of free expression and that I was extremely well qualified for the chairmanship of the NEH and ought to be confirmed. Even at this low ebb of my fortunes, I was not deserted by the people who knew me well. That gave me encouragement.

As I made my calls on the Committee Republicans, I found that minds were more open than the right wing wanted. Even Senator Dan Coates, perhaps the most conservative on the Committee, was willing to have a long and frank discussion with me on the issues, as was Judd Gregg, who is also quite conservative. Softened up by Lee Annenberg, Senator Thurmond looked at me through glazed eyes and assured me from behind his desk that he would read all my material and give me a fair hearing. Then he turned me over to his young assistant, who took me over the hurdles of all the charges that were by then being churned out by the conservative advocacy groups who were combing through the garbage at Penn for juicy tidbits that might nourish a lethally accusatory rodent or two. I had a chance to respond to each of them, and in the process to be alerted to the likely critique I would face at the confirmation hearing itself.

Senator Kassebaum was encouraging, as was Senator Hatch, but they would not commit themselves to support me. As Senator Kassebaum told me, "It is hard for me to commit to you if the White House is not committed." She meant that she would not think of announcing how she was going to vote until the papers for my nomination were formally delivered to the Senate Committee.

I asked Nestor why the nomination had not been sent up. It was simply hung up in the White House Counsel's Office, he replied. After about a week of courtesy calls, it became clearer that nothing was going to happen on the Hill until the nomination actually arrived. Nestor continued to tell me that it was simply hung up in the bureaucracy. I remembered that, earlier in the process, when I was feeling especially insecure, I thought that it might be a good idea for me to use my own money to hire a "consultant" with extensive Washington experience. I realized that this might appear to be a criticism of Howard Paster's operation in the White House, and I also imagined that he might not like to lose control of the process. I therefore went to see him, knowing that I was likely to hear that he did not want me to hire my own person. Indeed, that is what I heard. He told me not to worry, though. The White House was behind me. Besides, his wife was a particular fan of the humanities and he could not afford to let me fail because he would hear about it at home.

I was not particularly reassured, but I had no real option. I knew that I was prepared to be an exceptionally good chairman of the NEH, and I wanted very much to have that opportunity. At the same time, I understood that all White House politics are about the President and what is in his best interest. As important as the NEH is to the humanities in this country, it is not a very important agency in the politics of the federal government. I can imagine an advisor to the President saying, "It isn't worth spending any political capital on this appointment." It is also true that the fate of Western civilization was not riding on my confirmation. There were half a dozen eager and capable candidates who could do the job and whose nominations would be less politically costly. Just as the attack on me was not really about me, the White House's support of me was not really about me either.

Consequently, I went back to work, but the longer my nomination was "lost" in the "in-out-hold" boxes of the Counsel's office, the more suspicious I got. Finally, Nestor leveled with me. My nomination was being held up until the White House was sure I could win. What would convince them? We needed to get a Republican vote! So, I was in a catch-22. The Republicans on the Committee would not commit until the nomination was actually sent up to the Senate, and the White House wouldn't send the nomination up until I got at least one Republican to commit his or her support.

The nightmare began to transform itself quietly on June 10, just as all the visible signs were looking gloomy. I was in Washington at the Hay-Adams again, planning to go with Nestor to hammer some more pitons into the face of the Senatorial glacier. Melanne Verveer of the First Lady's office called as I was about to go down for a quick breakfast. Before joining the First Lady's staff, Melanne had worked with People for the American Way, a liberal advocacy group, and she eventually succeeded Maggie Williams as the First Lady's chief-of-staff. She knew her way around Washington, and I assume that she had been charged by Hillary Clinton to help me. The Office of the First Lady in the Old Executive Office Building (OEOB) had therefore become my home away from home. I could make telephone calls from there. When the conference room was not in use, I could camp out and study my NEH homework. The support of the First Lady's staff was beyond doubt, but they could only argue my case within the White House. They could not control other offices that were directly in charge.

"Have you seen the *New York Times*?" Melanne asked on June 10. My stomach began to churn with anxiety. Another attack. Rats! "It is good news," Melanne hurried on to say. "Get a copy." I did. The title of the editorial was "Don't Burn Hackney at the Stake." While it repeated a couple of the distortions of the *WSJ* campaign, it concluded that I was well qualified for the position of chairman of the NEH and that I should be confirmed. This was a significant breakthrough, especially inasmuch as the *Times* had opposed Lani Guinier. Furthermore, the timing could not have been better. I think that Sandy McCrary, the senior staff person for Senator Claiborne Pell's subcommittee that had jurisdiction over NEH and NEA authorization, had talked to a member of the *Times* editorial board to suggest that this would be a good time. It was. I owe Howell Raines and his colleagues a great deal for speaking out in my behalf at a critical time.

I assume that the *New York Times* endorsement gave some courage to my hometown paper, the *Philadelphia Inquirer*. It followed on June 13 in an editorial entitled, "Sheldon the Terrible? The Demonization of Penn's Hackney." The editorial confessed that the *Inquirer* had done its share of "pummeling," but now I was "being beaten to a pulp." "Things have gotten runaway ugly," it said, and then criticized the Clinton White House for not defending its candidate.

The rest of the day on June 10 was just as good as the beginning of it. I called on Senator Kennedy, who needed no sales pitch. In addition to the fact that he was prepared to fight the White House's fight on this symbolic front, my wife and I had met him several times over the years when he was visiting our next-door neighbors on the Vineyard, Rose Styron, the poet and human rights activist, and her husband William Styron, the novelist. In addition, Ted had married Vicki Reggie, the beautiful, brilliant, and charming daughter of a politically prominent Louisiana family connected to Tulane. Vicki and Lucy had been classmates at Tulane Law School.

After some brief pleasantries about our various connections, Ted began to talk tactics. When a vote was announced for one o'clock that day, he quickly arranged to use a reception room just off the Senate floor. I waited there while he brought Democrats to meet me. It was both thoughtful and useful. I met more than a dozen Senators that way. Even though it was fleeting, at least they could now associate a face with the name that they had been hearing terrible things about. It also made clear that Senator Kennedy was prepared to fight for my confirmation.

Later that afternoon, I went to see Senator John Danforth at the suggestion of Harris Wofford. Danforth had been a staunch supporter of Clarence Thomas during his confirmation battles for the Supreme Court. Thomas had once served on Danforth's staff, and they continued to be friends. Danforth himself came in for considerable criticism for sponsoring Thomas, and he was appalled and outraged at the vilification that had become part of the confirmation process. When Harris had spoken to Danforth on my behalf, Danforth had replied that he was already being lobbied incessantly for me. Even his brother, Bill, chancellor of Washington University in St. Louis, had called. Bill and I, naturally, had come to know each other very well through our work together as members of the American Association of Universities. Senator Danforth then told Harris that "he had a speech" that he was looking for an occasion to give, and this might be it.

I met with Senator Danforth at 5 P.M. We talked about my situation in particular and more generally about the bruising incivility and character assassination that had become typical of Washington politics. He eventually said that he had "been waiting for me," meaning he had been waiting for another nomination that would provide an occasion for him to denounce trial by publicity. Nestor went immediately back to his office and put together a package of information about me, the Water Buffalo incident, and the theft of newspapers for Danforth to use. We subsequently heard from third parties that one of Danforth's staff members was advising him not to support me. That may account for the call I got later from his office asking whether I had taken a position on Clarence Thomas during the Anita Hill hearing. I had not.

As I was leaving Danforth's office on Thursday, June 10, he drawled, "Well, I am your Republican vote." He promised to vote for me and to speak on the floor for me. Furthermore, he wanted to write an op-ed piece about the nomination process using me as an example. I was delighted.

When the op-ed appeared in the *Washington Post*, its opening sentence was, "If the president calls to say that he will nominate you for a job subject to confirmation by the Senate, just say no." It was focused on the "carnage of presidential nominations," the incivility of a process that no longer recognizes any limits, as people seek to use presidential nominations to make a political point, furthering a philosophical position, or "establishing our own moral superiority or embarrassing the president of the United States." He warned that the public was getting disgusted, "And that disgust will reflect our sense that those who have been nominated are more than stand-ins for political positions. They are human beings."

On the way to making that point, Senator Danforth noted that, "The next controversial nominee will be Sheldon Hackney . . . under fire for his 'politically correct' handling of various racial controversies during his presidency of the University of Pennsylvania." After noting how difficult college campuses were, Danforth wrote, "A case can be made that Hackney went too far in his efforts to placate outraged black students and that free expression suffered. But what is the purpose in raising this issue in the context of Hackney's nomination? . . . The attack on Hackney for his management of the University of Pennsylvania, while unrelated to the mission of the NEH, is directly related to the politically lucrative field of racial and ethnic divisiveness. If the racial turmoil of a university campus can be transported to Washington, the political benefits are enormous."[4]

On June 10, however, that was still in the future. I went back to the OEOB immediately and told Melanne that Danforth had promised his support, as I am sure Nestor also reported to Howard Paster. I was in Melanne's crowded little office. She immediately picked up the phone and called Paster. There ensued a vigorous discussion that I could barely get the drift of. Melanne was asking for the nomination to be sent up to the Senate immediately, and she was meeting resistance. She put the phone down and said, "Bill Galston is going to come down; he wants to talk to you."

Galston appeared promptly. He was a quiet, slight man with curly hair and glasses. He spoke very deliberately. I was not surprised to discover that he was a philosopher who had taught at the University of Maryland, and would eventually return there. As an academic, he was a principal theorist of the communitarian movement. Later, I read his books, along with those of Amitai Etzioni, with great interest and profit. He had also been a strategist for the Democratic Leadership Forum, the centrist group of which Bill Clinton was a leader, and he was now an assistant to the President. We sat facing each other on opposite ends of the parson's bench in Melanne's office and talked while she made phone calls.

Though I tried not to indicate it, I knew exactly what was going on. Danforth's promise of support had precipitated a "fish-

or-cut-bait" moment, as they say in my native region. Bill had been sent to quiz me and to make a judgment about whether it would be better to pursue the nomination or withdraw it. Three years later, after we had gotten to know each other a bit, Bill and I were together at a "civil society" conference in Prague, Czech Republic. Over a drink, I recalled this occasion and told him my suspicion. He confirmed it. He had been delegated to make the call for the President, and he was trying to satisfy himself that I and my story would stand up. In Melanne's office, he took me very meticulously through the events of the spring at Penn, as well as through some of the other accusations that had begun to be circulated by right wing think tanks, exploring not only my actions but my beliefs. It felt very much like the oral exam for my Ph.D. When Bill left, I did not know what his conclusion was. The next day, however, when I was back in my office at Penn, I learned from Melanne that she had succeeded in getting Howard Paster to agree to send the nomination up to the Senate on Monday, June 14. Bill Galston had decided that I and my story were worth backing.

Once my nomination went up to the Hill, Senator Kennedy quickly set the confirmation hearing for the morning of June 25, less than two weeks away. Eager as I was to get on with life, this put additional pressure on me at a particularly busy time of year. I had a party for my staff on the Saturday after Galston had grilled me and Melanne had prevailed on Howard Paster to take the risk and send my nomination along. That next week was full of preparations for my last set of Trustee meetings on Thursday and Friday, June 17 and 18.

My sporadic journal scribblings recorded my feelings after those final meetings. "The final trustee meetings a week ago (June 17 & 18) went well. Everyone was wonderful and complimentary. The party at the Morris Arboretum was a lot of fun on a beautiful evening. Fain was the star of the show, reading a humorous and touching statement about being the 'son of.' It was extremely good and I was very proud of him. The Trustees are endowing a chair in the History Department that will bear Lucy's and my name. That is a real kick. I have been spending most days in D.C. calling on Senators and going through mock hearings. As grueling as it was, it was necessary and useful. I was so keyed up and so exhausted that I was afraid that I would not perform well under pressure."

Al Shoemaker presided at the farewell dinner with his usual down-to-earth good humor. He kept the sentimentality to a minimum, while making everyone feel good about being engaged together in such a noble and successful effort as the University of Pennsylvania. It is also nice to be honored in front of one's children.

I spent my spare time that weekend writing my opening statement for the confirmation hearing that was to be the following Friday. I had already been in training for this event for some time, so I was eager as well as nervous. I remember in particular the mock hearing that Melanne Verveer staged as part of my training. It had been on June 3. In addition to Melanne around the table in the First Lady's conference room were Nestor, Martha Chowning from NEH, Ricki Seidman from the White House Press Office, Susan Clampitt from White House Personnel, the freelance lobbyist Liz Robbins, who had been amazingly effective with Democrats and Republicans alike, and perhaps a few more stand-ins for my senatorial tormentors. They fired the toughest questions they could imagine at me, and I was not terribly adept at answering in politically astute ways.

The group forced me through all the supposed scandals of my career. That took some time. A list of the controversial speakers I have defended would include, but would not be limited to, the following: William B. Shockley, the Nobel Laureate who was propounding racist genetic theories in the early 1970s; white students who wished to show *The Birth of a Nation* despite the anguished opposition of black students; King Hussein of Jordan, at a time when he was not the favorite world leader of Jewish students; Jerry Falwell, the evangelist who was a leader of the religious right; the student columnist who implied that Ronald Reagan had gotten what he deserved when he was shot; Ronald Reagan himself, when he appeared as part of Penn's 250th anniversary celebration, much to the dismay of ACT UP and activists for other causes; Louis Farrakhan; the Penn professor who burned an American flag as part of her class on communications; the Institute of Contemporary Art and the National Endowment for the Arts for the infamous Robert Mapplethorpe show. This partial list is enough to give one a headache, and it does not even touch the issues that roiled the Penn campus in the 1980s: South African investments, gay rights, women's rights, racial justice, security on campus, animal rights, and environmental activism. Each of these occasioned at least one major demonstration, sit-in, or protest during my time in office.

This stimulated a little revelation. It was the first time that I had noticed that it was possible to look at my career as a college president as one continuing emergency that careened from one crisis to the next. That is not the way I think of it. The real story is what the University was doing between crises. It is also true, I have come to think, that extraordinary results cannot be achieved without taking risks, and anyone pursuing a clear idea of what the university should be is bound to find himself dealing with conflicting values and with interest groups with ideas contrary to his. Crises are normal. The more serious immediate problem was how to keep the facts of so many crises straight, especially when my questioners would have been primed with the most hostile reading of those events.

Other than the usual sort of general advice (sit up straight, look them in the eye, appear confident but not cocky, don't be afraid to let your emotions show a little), the primary advice that came from this group is that I had to redefine myself for the Senate Committee. They and the public knew me mostly from the press coverage of the events in the spring, so they didn't know the real me. I had to let them see who I am. It was the hardest assignment I have ever had.

At one point in my rehearsal for the third degree, someone in the group said, "Mr. Hackney, looking at your record as a historian and as a college president, one is impressed, but Washington is a tough place, and I don't think you are tough enough to last here." In response, I quoted the immortal words of the late songwriter Jim Croce, "You don't tug on Superman's cape." Shattering the solemnity of the intensely serious session, that bit of mock bravado broke the group up.

"No, no, no," they said. "You can't say that! You have to be in command, it's true, but you have to be deferential at the same time. But, you are on the right track. You have been portrayed as a wimp, as the ineffectual, mild-mannered Clark Kent. You have to transform yourself into Superman—without a phone booth." I later received a framed cutout of Superman signed by Senator Kennedy and presented to me by my "handlers" at a post-confirmation celebration. It hangs on the wall in my study, a talisman of the rites of my initiation into the mysteries of political Washington.

5

AT LAST I SPEAK

S O, WHEN I was walking down the corridor on June 25 toward my appointment with Senator Kennedy and his committee, I had already been through my baptism of fire. This had long since ceased to be a rational calculation on my part about how much pain I was willing to suffer in order to get a job that I thought would be extremely interesting. It was now more of a determination not to let the bad guys win.

Events had been going in the right direction in the previous two weeks, but straws were being blown in various directions by the winds of public relations. The morning's *WSJ* contained a long editorial urging the Committee to turn me down. Charles Krauthammer devoted his column in the *Washington Post* that morning to arguing that I was the symbol of political correctness, so the Senate should turn my nomination into a referendum on political correctness. On the other hand, the *Post* also ran Jack Danforth's piece entitled, "A Presidential Nomination? Forget It." It was a wonderful boost, even though it was not really about me, and Harris Wofford inserted it into the record of my hearing.

The *Post* also endorsed me. At least, I think that is what it did. The editorial restated the charges against me in pretty much the same form that the *WSJ* would have used, but also put forward my experience and qualifications. This doesn't "add up to euphoria," the *Post* concluded, with a linguistic rhythm that sounded very much like Meg Greenfield herself, but it is good enough for confirmation.[1]

I remembered this squeaky endorsement four years later, after the NEH had survived the worst onslaught of the Republican revolution. The House subcommittee that had jurisdiction over the appropriations had just zeroed out the NEA but had voted a modest increase to cover inflation in the NEH's budget. The *Washington Times* reporter asked Ralph Regula why his subcommittee had treated the NEH so well. "Nobody is telling me they are doing anything terrible," he replied. I took that as a strong endorsement, given Ralph Regula's personality and the tenor of the times. Similarly, the *Post*'s grudging endorsement on the day of the hearing was a big help.

Martha Chowning and I worked our way forward from the door in the back of the room to the witness table in the front. The place was packed, and I knew that much of the audience was there for the same reason that people go to stock car races: to see the crash. There were some friendly faces as well. Melanne Verveer and several of my handlers from the White House were there, eager to see if I could follow directions. Rose Styron, Art Buchwald, Don and Ann Brown, Susan and Don Rappaport from among our Vineyard friends were up front and visible. Senator Kennedy allowed me to introduce my family members who were present: Lucy; our son, Fain; our daughter, Elizabeth McBride; her sister-in-law, Siobahn McBride; and Lucy's sister, Anne Lyon.

Harris Wofford was a member of the Committee, but he was also introducing me, as was Representative Tom Foglietta, who for years represented the district in which the University was located. Senators Howell Heflin and Richard Shelby from Alabama, my native state, had intended to be there to help introduce me but, as Senator Kennedy noted, the Senate had been in session late the night before and Heflin and Shelby had asked to be excused from appearing personally. The notable absence, of course, was Arlen Specter. It was not for lack of my trying. I licked boots, pulled my forelock, promised to sin no more, but Specter remained sulking in his tent.

The format was traditional. Wofford and Foglietta each made a statement. Each of the Senators on the Committee who were present (Kennedy, Pell, Kassebaum, Coats, and Hatch—with Wofford playing two roles) made introductory statements. Then, I was allowed to make my preliminary statement. That was followed by questioning by the Committee members in sequence. The statements by Wofford and Foglietta, by design, not only stressed my accomplishments and qualifications for the post, but leaned against the major themes of my critics: I was a champion of free speech, I was a knowledgeable critic of political correctness, I was a proven leader, I was a balanced and judicious administrator. The members of the Committee in their introductory statements generally tried to set the tone of the hearing by stressing the importance of the NEH and the importance for the NEH of having someone who was not a captive of political correctness. Senator Kennedy did not have to pretend to be neutral, and he wasn't.

In his initial remarks addressed to me, he made it clear that he was friendly. Senator Wofford takes pride in your nomination because you are from Pennsylvania, he said, "but we too in Massachusetts take a certain pride in your appointment. I know that you have the good sense and good judgment to spend a good deal of time up in Vineyard Haven, up on Martha's Vineyard." "Yes," I said, "I wish I were there now."

Kennedy responded, "Well, later, over the weekend, maybe—we won't make it too warm for you in here. [Laughter]" It was a huge help having Kennedy in the chair.

When my turn came to present my opening statement, I said:

Thank you very much Mr. Chairman. I am pleased to be here to talk about a great range of things and about the National Endowment for the Humanities. If I may, I would like to start by telling you something about myself, something about what I have done in my career, and then something about how I see the National Endowment for the Humanities.

At first glance, my life does not appear to be one that was ever in need of transformation, yet I can bear personal witness to the sort of personal transformation that I believe the humanities have the power to accomplish.

I was born and raised in Birmingham, Alabama, the third son of a thoroughly Methodist family that eventually included five sons, the offspring of a marriage that is now in its sixty-fourth year. My childhood was spent in the Great Depression and World War II, and I was acutely aware that my world was one of scarcity and vulnerability. Nevertheless, my childhood was unproblematic, at least if one doesn't count my being continuously terrorized by my older brothers.

My father was a newspaperman before the war. As that was not the era of the journalist as hero, and as his family was large, when he returned from the Navy he set himself up in business buying and reselling war surplus material. His business evolved and he eventually did very well.

As I went through public school in Birmingham, like most children of middle-income families, I could imagine various futures for myself, each of them honorable and productive, but I never imagined the life I have actually had. That life was opened up for me in part because of two superb History teachers at Ramsay High School, Mary McPhaul and Ellen Callen, and in part because I loved to read.

My mother read to us a lot when we were young, and when I was a bit older I remember listening wondrously to her practicing the dramatic readings that she did for literary clubs around the city, legitimate theater not having a very lively presence in Birmingham then. Although reading was a bit of magic for me, I was thoroughly imprisoned in the myth that real boys did not work very hard in school and real men were men of action rather than thought.

The major reason, however, that the world was saved from having yet another lawyer was my older brother, Fain, whom I worshipped. He was charismatic and multi-talented and very imaginative, so that he was always the leader in the neighborhood and the one who would organize our play, not only the standard games like kick-the-can and hide-and-seek, but elaborate war games and a game we called "town" in which everyone had a role selling something, and Fain was always the banker because he could draw so well and make beautiful dollar bills. My brother, Morris, always got the lemonade concession and ended up with all the money that Fain issued from the bank.

Fain was a young man of grandiose projects, usually too grand ever to finish but always exciting enough to draw in everyone else. Despite all his talent, he had an uneven academic record, reflecting his enthusiasms and his lack of focus, but he had a great time and made all those around him have a great time also. He went off to the University of Alabama where parties were then known to occur. He had a wonderful time his freshman year, and his abysmal grades showed it.

Something happened to him that following summer, and I don't know what the transforming event or experience was. In any case, he became a different person. He started reading books that were not required for school. He began to listen to classical music, to write poetry, and to talk of serious subjects. He transferred to Birmingham-Southern College and started to work at his courses. I was fascinated.

Part of his plan for remaking his life was to become a Navy

pilot, which he did. When I went off to Vanderbilt on a Naval ROTC scholarship, he was on the west coast and then in Japan flying amphibious patrol planes. Letters from him were not only reports of adventures in exotic places but accounts of what he was reading and thinking, and guilt-producing questions about my intellectual life, which even at Vanderbilt could be as sparse as one wanted it to be.

It was at about this time, because of Fain's example if not his specific recommendation, that I was captured by the novels of William Faulkner, Ernest Hemingway, and especially Thomas Wolfe. I am almost embarrassed to remember how much I identified with Eugene Gant, a young Southerner coming of age by trying to read his way through the Harvard library. Vanderbilt was saturated, of course, with the tradition of the Fugitive poets and the Agrarians, and I studied them with appreciation. Though the Agrarians had taken their stand twenty years before in very different times, and had since then taken diverse political paths, the big questions they had raised (about what is the good life, and what is the value of tradition, and what is the function of government, and what are the perils of modernity) were common and lively topics of debate among my friends.

We also talked of race relations, an omnipresent concern of Southerners black and white that was intensified by the Supreme Court's ruling in the *Brown* case that put an exclamation mark in the middle of my college years. For reasons that I find difficult to explain, but that probably have to do with my religious training, I had broken away from Southern white orthodoxy even before going to college and had concluded that racial segregation was wrong. As a historian, I have continued my interest in race because it is a major factor in American history. As an individual, I have continued my commitment to racial equality because I believe it is right and that group relationships are one of the major unresolved questions on the domestic scene. In the formal curriculum at Vanderbilt, Dewey Grantham, Herb Bailey, and Henry Swint in the History department increased my interest in History.

I was devastated by the death of my brother in a military plane crash in Japan in 1954 during the summer after my sophomore year. He had meant so many things to me that it was not until years later that I realized that his most important gift to me was to give me permission to use my mind in serious ways, to risk pursuing a subject that I enjoyed, to spend my life in pursuit of education for myself and for others. Watching him change, and being lured into the pleasures of thought as a way of enhancing experience, transformed my life and gave it purpose.

After three years on a destroyer and two years teaching weapons at the United States Naval Academy in Annapolis, I went to Yale to study under C. Vann Woodward, the leading historian of the South and the man who became the most important influence on my career as a historian and on my devotion to academic freedom, intellectual honesty, free speech, and the obligations of collegiality. I had been attracted to Woodward not only by his reinterpretation of the history of the South from Reconstruction to World War I, but by his subtle exploration, in the essays collected in *The Burden of Southern History*, of what it means to be a Southerner and what the history of the South means to the nation and the world.

After Yale, I joined the faculty of Princeton, where I worked away at becoming the best teacher and scholar I could possibly be, while raising a family and doing the sort of committee assignments and quasi-administrative tasks that faculty are called upon to do. My career as a historian, in fact, was diverted because I kept saying yes to such requests. When William G. Bowen became President of Princeton in 1972, he invited me to become Provost. The slippery slope turned into a water chute. I became President of Tulane University in 1975 and of the University of Pennsylvania in 1981. This confirms the truth of the aphorism that life is what happens to you while you are planning something else.

I believe my twenty years of major responsibility in universities has prepared me to lead the National Endowment for the Humanities. For the past generation, universities have provided tough environments. University presidents operate in a sea of powerful and conflicting currents. To succeed, one must have a clear sense of strategic direction, a fundamental commitment to the core values of the university, the strength to persevere through contentious times, and the ability to gain and keep the support of a variety of constituencies. I have not only survived in that environment, I have prospered and my institutions have thrived.

Among the values that I hold dear is a belief that a university ought to be open to all points of view, even if some of those views expressed are personally abhorrent. I take some pride in having protected the right to speak of such diverse controversial figures as William Shockley at Princeton, King Hussein of Jordan at Tulane, and Louis Farrakhan at Penn. The university should belong to all of its members and not be the exclusive domain of any particular person, group, or point of view.

During my twelve and a half years at Penn, I have made the undergraduate experience my highest priority. Penn has revamped the general education components of the curriculum in each of its four undergraduate schools, provided a livelier sense of community through the creation of freshman houses within the residential system, added a reading project that asks freshmen to read a common book and then to discuss that book in seminars during orientation week and throughout the year, revised our advising system, revitalized the freshman seminar program, and drawn senior faculty into the teaching of introductory courses. I have increased the diversity of the Penn student body and worked hard to sustain an inclusive and supportive atmosphere on campus, to provide a campus in which everyone has a very strong sense of belonging and in which our animated debates are carried out with civility. I have also created a new sense of partnership with the neighborhoods around us, a close working relationship with the school system of the City of Philadelphia, and a national model program of volunteerism that I institutionalized a year ago by establishing the Center for Community Partnerships to stimulate and coordinate the involvement of faculty, staff and students in off-campus service activities.

Universities exist to create new knowledge and to preserve and communicate knowledge. The NEH, as a sort of university without walls, through its research, education, and public programs, is engaged in the same effort. I am dedicated to the proposition that we can improve the human condition through knowledge, and that our hope for tomorrow in this troubled world depends on the sort of understanding that can come through learning.

I have great respect for the NEH. It is the single most important institution in American life promoting the humanities, and it has a long record of accomplishment. I believe there are things that can be done to extend and broaden the impact of the NEH as it fulfills its statutory task of stimulating the humanities.

I like to think of the humanities as human beings recording and thinking about human experience and the human condition, preserving the best of the past and deriving new insights in the present. One of the things that the NEH can do is to conduct a national conversation around the big questions: what is the meaning of life, what is a just society, what is the nature of duty, and so on. In this big conversation, it is not the function of the NEH to provide answers but to insure a discussion, to create a forum in which all voices can be heard.

Because they are not just for the few but for everyone, no single approach to the NEH mandate is adequate. There is a need for balance among research aimed at creating new knowledge, educational programs to insure that the humanities are creatively and invitingly represented in the curricula of our schools and colleges, and public programs to draw everyone into the big conversation. Those three activities should be related to each other and should be mutually supportive.

The country has never needed the humanities more. We not only face the challenges of a new geopolitical situation, and the problems of adjusting to economic competition in a new global marketplace, but we face a crisis of values at home. What is happening to family and community? Who are we as a nation and where are we going? What holds us together as a nation and what do citizens owe to each other? What is the relationship of the individual to the group in a society whose political order is based upon individual rights and in which group membership is still a powerful influence?

Even more importantly, the humanities have the capacity to deepen and extend to new dimensions the meaning of life for each and every one of us. They have the capacity to transform individual lives, not necessarily in the external circumstances of those lives, but in their internal meaning.

Every human experience is enhanced by higher levels of knowledge. When I listen to a piece of music, I may like it and think it is beautiful, but the person who knows the historical context of its composition, understands what the composer was trying to accomplish technically, and can compare the composition and the performance to others will get infinitely more out of the experience than I will. That is why I enjoy talking about common experiences with people who will see it through a lens different from mine. The task of the NEH is to enrich the conversation and bring more people into it.

The premise of my approach to the tasks of the National Endowment for the Humanities is simple but profound. The more you know, the more you hear and see and feel. The more you know, the more you can know. The more you know, the more meaningful life is. Such can be the gift of the NEH to the American people.

When it came Senator Kassebaum's turn to question me, she said, "Dr. Hackney, I have heard many confirmation statements, and I would just like to say I don't know that I have ever heard one that was more beautifully written, and obviously by quite a fine writer." I replied, "Thank you very much. It is from the heart, Senator." And it was.

6

THE GRILLING

EVEN THOUGH I had poured out my heart in my statement, it did not save me from being grilled by the members of the Committee. I understood that in good political science theory I ought to be thankful that I was going to be asked the toughest questions imaginable. That would allow me to get my answers on the record, which would provide the basis—theoretically—for the deliberations of the full Senate, for which the Committee was—theoretically—doing the staff work. In real life, however, I wanted the Committee to say, "Hey, that's good enough for me. Let's go to lunch."

It was not to be. It was, though, comforting to have Ted Kennedy in the chair. Knowing that he was trying to help me gave me confidence. By prerogative, he had the first turn at asking questions. He threw me big, fat, slow, straight pitches over the heart of the plate. He asked me to tell the Committee about the two controversial cases at Penn in the spring. With very little prompting from him, I then got a chance to tell the stories of the Water Buffalo incident and the theft of the newspapers.

Somehow, as I told the stories, they didn't sound as outrageously un-American as when they were told by the *Wall Street Journal.* I was able to provide both the facts, free of polemical

twists, and my own opinions about those facts. So, I was able to
stress how I thought I had been clear in my condemnations of the
theft of the newspapers, how the students involved in that event
still faced University disciplinary action, and how I had thought it
inappropriate to intervene in the judicial process with regard to the
Water Buffalo incident.

Kennedy helped. "We in the Senate are often asked to intervene in legal proceedings when it appears that an injustice may have
been done. We generally decline to do so because we recognize the
importance of allowing the legal proceedings to take their course,
and then when they are concluded, we in the Senate can review
those proceedings to see if reforms are appropriate. So this is what
the Senators do, and it appears to me that is exactly what you did
at the university." "Indeed," I said, thinking that a light bulb
should be appearing over the heads of innocent observers, if there
were any.

With regard to the Water Buffalo case, I tried to summarize the
lessons that I had drawn from it. "One of the things that I come
away with is the fact that although I believe civility is extremely
important on the campus, and although I think we ought to have
a statement of standards, if you will, a policy, that tells students that
we expect them to behave with some civility with regard to other
people on the campus and not use racial slurs, I believe it is a
mistake to try to enforce that with punishments that are arrived at
through some adversarial student judicial process. It just doesn't
work very well and ought not to be tried."

Senator Nancy Kassebaum, as the ranking minority member,
had the second shot at me. She was also helpful, if it is a help to be
given a chance to respond to accusations of a nebulous sort. She
began by saying that the *WSJ* had charged that morning that I "had
compiled a record of appeasement in line with the prevailing
political winds." She wanted to know if it were true.

"Absolutely not," I replied. "I think throughout my career,

from the very beginning, I have been devoted to free speech on campus—open inquiry, I would say would be a better term for it—because I refer here not only to allowing controversial speakers to speak, but indeed, making sure the campus was open to all points of view in the free forum that is there.

"But I have also been very concerned about the ethics of teaching, if you will—that is, teachers, I believe, who are covering sensitive subjects should make sure that alternative points of view are presented to the students so the students can make up their own minds. That is certainly the way I teach, and in a statement of standards that I helped to draft for the American Historical Association, that was a feature as well."

Senator Kassebaum then asked the toughest question that a chair of the NEH or NEA has to face. She wanted to know whether I would turn down a grant proposal that had been recommended to me if the content of the activity being funded seemed "inappropriate" for the use of tax dollars. This was the Serrano and Mapplethorpe question, and I knew what she was driving at, but it is difficult to ask the question precisely without making it clear that you are asking about censorship. Shortly later, Senator Pell asked the same question in the same way. I also knew that a full and precise exposition of my position would put me at odds with most members of Congress, including some of the firmest friends of the two endowments. Consequently, I said simply that I would make sure the quality review process was rigorous and had integrity, and that I understood that the chair was totally responsible for each grant and that I was prepared to make tough decisions and to be held accountable. I am grateful that Senator Kassebaum did not press deeper into the subject.

The Supreme Court is very clear on this subject, and I believe it is right. The government is not obligated to provide subsidies for cultural activities (*e.g.*, NEA and NEH), but if it does, it may not discriminate on the basis of the content of the speech that is being sponsored. In short, if Mapplethorpe's photographs, by some objective criteria of quality, merit support in the competition for funding, then the NEA or NEH may not refuse to make the grant because the Chairman does not think the ideological or moral content is "appropriate" for the use of tax dollars. The Court has said that the government must not fund "obscenity," which has a definition based on community standards, but other than obscenity, the government may not choose among projects based on the content of the speech in that project.

This does not please a lot of members of Congress, left or right, who argue in effect, "You can say anything you want, but when tax dollars are involved you may not say or show things that would offend taxpayers." How many and which taxpayers is never specified.

The liberal rejoinder, obviously, is that some taxpayers are always seeing their money used for purposes of which they do not approve. Pacifists don't have the right to stop the government from spending on the national defense. Environmentalists don't have the right to stop government from building highways. In countless ways, we all pay our taxes and see them used in ways we would not personally approve.

From Senator Jesse Helms on the right to Senator Claiborne Pell on the left, for reasons of pragmatism or ideology, members of the Senate were eager to have a chairman of the NEH who would be "strong," meaning someone who would use his power to deny grants to projects that would cause political problems by offending some significant and vocal group. Proponents of this view say that when tax dollars are used, the project should be within some difficult-to-define mainstream.

Fortunately, I was not forced to go through this argument in great detail, because I am on the side of the Supreme Court. My assurance that I was prepared to be strong and expected to be held accountable was taken as an encrypted promise that I would not give a grant that would cause trouble. The irony did not escape me that the same Senators who were bashing me for being "wimpy" on free speech at Penn were asking me to wink and promise to be a surreptitious censor as the chairman of the NEH.

Perhaps the thoroughly well intentioned peroration of Senator Coats shortly later in the hearing captures the unconsciously schizophrenic character of this stance. "I would hope that should you be nominated," Senator Coats said, "you could diligently champion the rights of free speech, the rights of expression, regardless of which side of the political spectrum it came from. Having said that, you are put in the unenviable position of exercising judgment and restraint because we are utilizing taxpayers' funds, and that separates it, in my opinion. So that is a tough balance to find, and I am hopeful that you can walk through that mine field."

Senator Kassebaum also gave me a chance to talk about my attitude toward political correctness, which was then the smear of choice among ideological conservatives. I had written an op-ed column for the *Philadelphia Inquirer*, October 3, 1991, building on the remarks I had made at Commencement the preceding May, which had been published as usual in the *Almanac*. My major point in the op-ed was that political correctness did exist and was present on college campuses, but that it was not dominant and was not unchallenged. The term, with roots among the Marxist Left of the 1930s, had begun being used in self-derision by people on the Left on campus in the 1980s. It was meant to poke fun at the excessive concern about not using terminology that might be offensive to members of "oppressed groups." It quickly was expanded to cover any attitudes or actions that were somehow at odds with a supposed left-wing orthodoxy that favored the interests of previously oppressed groups or of progressive causes more generally. The term, "politically correct," was just as quickly co-opted by the Right as a way of charging the Left with authoritarianism.

As I looked at campus politics in 1991, there was a faction that was serious in its political correctness. There was also a faction of bitterly opposed folks on the Right. Most faculty and students, however, including me, were somewhere between those two extremes, trying to find reasonable ways to face a changing world.

To my mind, there were three different kinds of political correctness. First, there were people who wanted to use the university consciously as an instrument of political action. I have always been against this, and in the op-ed I expressed my support for the traditional ethic that teaching should not be indoctrination. Second, there were people who argued that every statement is a political statement, so the question was not "is the statement true," but "whose interests does it serve." To that, I said that truth might be impossible to achieve in any ultimate sense, but that it was essential to test truth claims against evidence and logic. If one did that, some statements would be revealed to be more true than others. Furthermore, the situational differences that appear to separate people from each other can be bridged through effort and rationality. Third, the big debate between multiculturalists on the Left, and traditionalists on the Right, about the importance of the Western tradition in the curriculum was viewed by most humanists as just another iteration in the constant debate over the content of the canon. As such, it should be resolved through compromises that preserved the centrality of the Western tradition but that opened the curriculum up to works from global, non-Western, and minority American traditions as well.

It is perfectly natural for political correctness, critical theory, deconstruction, post-structuralism, and post-modernism to be present on college campuses, just as every major intellectual movement ought to be represented and debated on the campus. What do you do, however, when any orthodoxy, especially an authoritarian orthodoxy, threatens to become dominant? This raises the paradox of the need to be tolerant of intolerance but only up to an unspecified point, and to allow no exclusive orthodoxy to control the campus, except for the orthodoxy of intellectual tolerance. I suspect that is a level of irony and subtlety that is not appropriate for a Senate hearing.

Senator Kassebaum apparently thought so too. As I was blathering on about political correctness, deconstruction, and post-structuralism, she interrupted. "I am only smiling, Dr. Hackney, because I couldn't help but think as you were talking about this how I am grateful we don't get into this on the Senate floor. We'd still be on the budget if that were the case." [laughter]

Senator Pell quizzed me about one of his pet ideas, the wisdom of weaving the state humanities councils more into the "warp and woof" of the life of the state by providing some official connection between them and the state governments. State humanities councils were private, self-perpetuating, non-profit organizations. I danced around that notion, not really liking it but not wanting to oppose a favorite idea of the founder of the NEA and NEH before I had even gotten into office. I replied that I was fundamentally opposed to the NEH being involved in any way with partisan or ideological politics, but that I would turn my attention to the state humanities councils and how to reach a broader public if I were confirmed. That was commitment enough for him, and he ended with a camouflaged encouragement like Senator Kassebaum's to use my power as chairman to turn down projects that might be offensive or controversial.

Senator Coats gave me less wiggle room, but was extraordinarily fair, especially in view of the fact that he did not like my politics at all. He got into the details of the two cases, indicating that he had spent some time thinking and preparing. "Why," he wanted to know, "had a request for a postponement of the disciplinary hearing from Eden Jacobowitz been turned down when, shortly afterward, a similar request from the women complainants had been granted?" My response was that I did not know because I was not involved and had no control over the process. I then explained that a university was highly decentralized, with authority delegated down through the president, provost, and deans to various faculty and student groups for specific functions. This is the concept of "shared governance" that is difficult for outsiders to understand because it is so different from the "command structures" that one finds in real life.

Penn had a very democratic ethos in its campus politics. Indeed, for reasons lost in history, faculty and student politicos seemed predisposed to oppose the president and the administration on principle. I remember in my early years at Penn telling the faculty senate that I believed in "shared governance"; I simply wanted the faculty to share some of it with me. They didn't seem to be amused.

Shared governance must have struck Senator Coats as mumbo jumbo. He said, "While that may be true of the way universities are structured today, no one in ultimate command or in charge—" "Well," I broke in, "that's not quite what I said, Senator." That got us back on track. He asked me how that system would compare to the role of the chairman of the NEH. "A completely different system," I was able to say. Indeed, by statute, the chairman of the NEH is solely responsible for each grant. All of the multi-tiered quality review is merely advisory. Of course, if you overrule the advice too often, you cause people to be unwilling to spend serious time giving good advice. Furthermore, when you don't do what the merit review system recommends, you are inviting the question, "Why not?"

Senator Coats invited me to draw a lesson from my experiences with Penn's student judicial system. I seized the opportunity to advise trustees nationally to review the delegation of authority in their university and to make sure the president and administrative officers had mechanisms through which they could be involved earlier in cases of student and faculty misconduct. The Penn system was not good, and I had set up a trustee-faculty-student group to review the events of the spring and make recommendations about how to improve the system. The result of that review the following year was the alteration of the system in the direction that I was indicating here.

Senator Coats then sought to undermine my position that it would not have been proper for me to intervene in the Jacobowitz case by pointing out that I had intervened in the Pavlik case. My position involves making a particular distinction and being aware of the narrative of the two cases, and it has bothered a lot of observers. In the Pavlik case, the charges had not been initiated when my assistant had called to inquire about the case. In fact, I did not known at the time of my Senate hearing what prompted the JIO not to proceed against Pavlik. Much later, while I was writing this account, I learned that the JIO had never intended to proceed against Pavlik but was drawing the process out in order not to offend the complaining black students. In fact, the JIO had already written to the complainants when my assistant inquired. The Jacobowitz matter came to my attention later in the spring of 1993. By the time my assistant made inquiries, the formal procedures had already been initiated. I suppose the JIO might have decided to change direction even then, but I was not empowered to order her to do so, but I had not ordered the dropping of the investigation of Pavlik either.

Senator Coats then tried to understand why I did not think that I had intervened later in the process when I had urged the JAO to try to hold the Jacobowitz hearing before the term was over rather than letting it be held over for the fall. Here again, I had no power to order the JAO to do anything, but I was not interfering in the substance of the case simply by pressuring the JAO to get the case before a faculty-student judicial panel. Though I did not say so at my confirmation hearing, when the panel finally held its ill-fated hearing, only to discover that the JAO had promised Kors that it would only consider his motion for dismissal and not the substance of the case, the panel took charge, and there was then nothing that I, the JAO or the JIO could do to influence its treatment of the case.

I have never liked such elaborately formalized disciplinary procedures, and the Jacobowitz case is a prime example of how the old-fashioned system of "dean's justice" would have been better. In the "old days," whether good or not, the dean simply summoned an offending student into his (inevitably male) office, listened to the excuses and explanations, and then decided what to do. Of course, advocates of procedural due process would point out that giving a "dean" the discretion to provide substantive justice, taking into account the offense, the offender, and the educational circumstances, is also giving him or her the discretion to provide injustice, to be arbitrary, and to be oppressively prejudiced. That is true; it is a risky trade-off, but it is one that I would probably make.

Senator Coats then asked about the charge leveled by journalists that I was observing a double standard, having proceeded against Jacobowitz but having not proceeded against the newspaper thieves even though I had disciplined the police involved in the apprehension of the thieves. "Senator," I replied, "I despair about the press." I then tried to explain how the disciplinary process was still in motion with regard to the students who had taken the newspapers. A special judicial investigative officer had been appointed to handle the case. A "judicial hold" had been put on the records of the one senior who was involved, and all the other students were in jeopardy. The security personnel, obviously, were not covered by faculty and student procedures. An administrative task force had been set up and was proceeding quickly to assess the charges that excessive force had been used (one apprehended student was struck with a billy club and several were handcuffed) and that the police had violated our own procedures when dealing with students. Frankly, it is easy to see why even an observer with the best intentions might have trouble understanding the niceties of university procedures with regard to different categories of people, and not all observers had good intentions.

Senator Coats then said that he liked my response to Senator Kassebaum about political correctness. It is unfortunate, he said, that I had become a symbol of political correctness. The only good part of that was that I was serving to bring an important issue before the public; the bad part was that it was not fair that my nomination should be judged on its symbolic value. He was not going to do that. I greatly respected him for that.

I responded at length, saying that my eighteen years as a college president had prepared me to make tough judgments under great pressure and to remain centered on my basic principles while applying common sense: "I also am very pleased that you said what you did about political correctness and my role in stimulating the debate. If I can be of service to the nation in stimulating an important debate, that's a good thing. But I must say I resent bitterly being victimized and slandered by slogan, and I hope that in the process of the hearing, which is one of the reasons that I am glad to be here, that I will be able to clear up something about who I am. I am not just a cardboard figure. I am someone who has spent a career defending free speech and will do that in the National Endowment for the Humanities as well."

Senator Hatch's interrogation began disarmingly, and then re-ferred to our long conversation in his office. Because of that, he said he was sympathetic, but he resented the injustice of the defeat of Carol Iannone's nomination to the National Council of the Hu-manities. He said he was going to give me an "opportunity" to answer the *Wall Street Journal*'s accusations. I became apprehen-sive. Wasn't this a ploy used by Perry Mason in those mysteries that I consumed while growing up. There is always a trap there some-where, just when you least expect it.

I got more apprehensive as the questions got more friendly.

Senator Hatch read from the *WSJ* editorial of the morning and said, "It is easy to sit back and pick some isolated instances where you are dealing with a very, very tough academic community; you've got wild-eyed professors on both sides of the issue; you've got people who are academically unbelievable teaching these kids today—you know it, I know it—and you've got a lot of people who really just want that university to do the very best it can for those students. They are the vast majority, and I think most university presidents are in that category; they want to do what is right. How do you handle that? What about these procedures? Don't you think you have an obligation to insert yourself and say, 'Hey, look, the procedure is wrong. This is infringing on free speech.'"

Warily I restated my position that it would be neither wise nor fair to interfere with the process while the case was in progress. Senator Hatch responded, "Why wait for next year?" Well, I said, "you really must bring everyone else along." "Do you mean to tell me," Hatch broke in, "if you don't bring everyone else along, you are going to have even more problems than if not?" "I think it is better, yes," I said, "to develop this consensus here." Then I pointed out that I had already said that the policy needed changing and that I had appointed a commission that would look at the process and suggest changes next year."

Hatch was suspicious, but reverted back to the *WSJ* editorial's accusation that I had exonerated the students in the newspaper theft because they were involved in a protest activity. I denied that charge and said that I thought I had been clear in my statement at the time of the incident. Hatch read from my controversial "two-values-in-conflict" statement and said, "I think it is a good statement." Then I really got nervous. What was he up to?

Hatch read from the end of the statement where I say that any violations of University policy will be "investigated according to established University procedures." Then he asked, innocently, "And you felt obligated to follow those procedures as University

president." "I did," I said, "yes." There then followed an exchange
about why I thought it best to follow procedures. I answered but
was still looking for the trap door.

> Senator Hatch: All right. If I were the University president,
> I might feel a little bit the same way you did. I might want to
> respect the procedure a little bit, too, realizing it is there, it may
> not be right, and we may have to change it—but at least it's there,
> and you can't just unilaterally overrule it, since it involves the
> faculty, the students, and almost everybody else involved with the
> institution, right?
> Mr. Hackney: Exactly. Right.
> Senator Hatch: It is easy to criticize on isolated instances. I
> have no doubt about that. And I am not trying to give you an easy
> time here.
> Mr. Hackney: I have no doubt about that. [Laughter]
> Senator Hatch: I am a powder puff, I know that. [Laughter]

My defenses were still up. Hatch led me through a series of
exchanges and got me to say that I was "trying to cultivate having
African American students and other minority students on campus, right?" "The task is not simply to cultivate African American
students," I said defensively. "Well," said Hatch, "to give them the
opportunity to be there and get an education at Penn—" "Absolutely," I said.

Then Hatch talked about the need on campuses like Ivy
League campuses to make African American students feel at home,
because they feel singled out by police, for instance, and the
university has to work hard to make them understand their feelings
will be taken seriously by the university, and some of them come
from disadvantaged backgrounds and may have a chip on their
shoulder, and anticipate that they will not be treated fairly.

I was very worried now. This was either an excellent grasp of the situation or a trap about to be sprung. I thought the only reason he could be bringing it out was to then produce an irrefutable argument about why it was the wrong way to see the situation. Nevertheless, he got me to say that it was a matter of great concern to me.

Senator Hatch: It should be. It should be. I think the other Ivy League schools ought to be concerned, too, and they ought to do it outside of the realm of quotas and ought to be doing it by searching out the best students and getting them there, and giving them the opportunity.

Mr. Hackney: I couldn't agree more.

Senator Hatch: But there is no question that that is a reality, isn't it?

Mr. Hackney: Absolutely, yes.

Senator Hatch: And you have to face it in the inner city of Philadelphia, right?

Mr. Hackney: Yes.

Senator Hatch: And the University of Pennsylvania is right in the middle of Philadelphia, isn't it?

Mr. Hackney. It is. It is in —

Senator Hatch: It isn't in the elite section of Philadelphia, is it—and you may feel that it is, but I have been there —

Mr. Hackney: It is an urban garden, Senator. [Laughter.]

Senator Hatch: Now I can see why it is going to be impossible to reject you in the Senate because you have such a way with words. But let me go a little further here. I don't like the police being singled out, either. They must feel a little bit insular themselves, because they are always picked on every time there is a criticism.

Mr. Hackney: We need them.

Senator Hatch: That's right. In other words, having them investigated doesn't mean you are going to crush them or turn around and trample them, does it?

Mr. Hackney: Absolutely not.

Senator Hatch: You are going to make sure their rights are protected.

Mr. Hackney: Yes.

Senator Hatch: Well, I have to say I think your statement could have been a little less mushy.

Mr. Hackney: Others have said the same thing—some members of my own faculty.

Senator Hatch: Keep in mind that comes from a former janitor, though, so it is easy for me to say that.

Mr. Hackney: That was also done in the heat of combat, if you will.

Senator Hatch: And it is pretty extensive, too—I mean, there is a lot of stuff in here that someone could try to split hairs on.

Mr. Hackney: Yes.

Senator Hatch went on to say that he would have preferred that my statement condemn the newspaper thefts more unequivocally, but that he understood that I needed to try to balance things so as to keep the campus together. Other college presidents, he thought, would have done the same thing. Then he cited the *WSJ* editorial's criticism of me as lacking in courage and leadership, and he commented that what might count as leadership in some settings would not fly at a university.

For my part, I admitted that if I could do it over again, I would craft my statement to be more clear in its commitment to free speech and less amenable to distortion. I wish I had thought to point out then, or at some time during the whole horror show, that the correct question to ask was not whether that particular statement was clear enough in its defense of free speech, but whether I had left anyone at Penn in doubt about the theft of newspapers being a violation of University regulations. Given the fact that two other unmistakable statements from me appeared on the same *Almanac* page as the broader statement about the state of race relations, I think the answer to that question is that everyone at Penn understood from me that the theft of newspapers was wrong and that the University would proceed against the perpetrators. Of course, the *WSJ* and those who followed its lead never reported the whole of the allegedly ambiguous statement, much less the whole of the *Almanac* page containing my communications to the campus. This is a case of telling a large lie with little truths.

Senator Hatch next asked about an accusation being widely circulated having to do with a teacher, Murray Dolfman. His class had been interrupted by black students who were angry because he had humiliated them in front of the class for not being able to explain the Thirteenth Amendment. Dolfman, an adjunct professor in the Wharton School, was not rehired for the succeeding year and then required to attend a "sensitivity" workshop before he taught again. The accusation was that treating him in this way was political correctness gone mad. My response was that whatever one thinks about the merits of humiliation as a pedagogical technique (and I do not like it), it was his department and not I who disciplined him. Hatch understood.

Then Senator Hatch brought up the letter signed by sixteen Penn law faculty criticizing my "two-values-in-conflict" statement. It was being used as evidence by my opposition that even my own faculty was opposed to me. Hatch read the entire letter, then he asked two questions. First, do I agree that the theft of the newspapers struck at the central value of the University. I, of course, do agree with that. Then he asked me why I resorted to the balancing rhetoric of my statement, even though he had just explained that beautifully himself.

In response, I said that I did not want the grievance of the black students to be completely lost, even though I thought and said that the theft was a violation of University regulations and that free speech was the paramount value of the university. I could have said it more clearly, and said it in a way that was less susceptible to misinterpretation. My interrogator accepted that.

Senator Hatch ended by saying he would love to go into my criticisms of the Helms Amendment, which he thought were wrong, and that he hoped that I understood that there were some sorts of projects that were not appropriate for the use of tax dollars, and that he resented the defeat of Carol Iannone's nomination. Nevertheless, he said, I had been criticized unfairly, that he appreciated my responses to the questions that had been put to me, and that he intended to support me. I exhaled at last.

Round two began with Senator Kennedy throwing me another softball: What about Penn's relationships to the city? There, I had a good-news story to tell, and I talked for ten minutes or more about all the things Penn was now doing in the city and in West Philadelphia. That was fun.

Senator Kassebaum brought up Penn's problems with indirect cost recoveries on research contracts. This is an arcane topic that had been converted into gripping news by Congressman John Dingell's crucifixion of Stanford, making it seem as if Stanford had made the government pay for a presidential yacht and other accouterments of high living. As soon as that story broke, of course, Penn and every other sensible research university checked its books to see how it would do if hostile federal investigators came snooping. We found that, indeed, the expenses of running the president's residence on campus at Penn had been coded as belonging to the pool of central administrative costs that were partially recovered by being allocated to research contracts, depending on the ratio of total direct research costs to total educational costs. It was never true that all of the flowers for parties at the president's house were paid for by the government, as newspaper accounts implied, but it was true at Penn, and elsewhere, that our accountants were aggressive in classifying costs that were put into the central cost pool, a portion of which got paid through indirect cost recovery.

At Penn, we decided immediately to reclassify and take out of the indirect cost pool all costs that would be hard to explain to the public, including the president's house. Consequently, we gave back to the federal government $930,000. That can be made to sound like a lot of money, but as Bob Atwell, president of the American Council on Education, explained in a letter-to-the-editor of *Time* magazine, it amounted to less than one tenth of one percent of the federal research dollars that went to Penn over the five years in question. That satisfied our department of Health and Human Services auditors, and it satisfied Senator Kassebaum. Most of the audience was asleep by the time I finished talking about indirect cost recovery formulas.

Senator Kassebaum closed with friendly remarks. I especially appreciated her saying that it was clearly very easy at a university or at the NEH for the person in charge to get pushed around by the pressures unless that person had a firm direction. Furthermore, she said that, as she listened to my answers with regard to the Penn problems of the spring, she had concluded that the president ought not to be involved in individual disciplinary cases. I took these comments to be an endorsement of my course of action on the campus in the spring of 1993. She concluded that that same firm sense of direction would be needed at the NEH because there would be pressures there as well to depart from guidelines and established procedures. "That is excellent advice that I will take," I replied.

Senator Pell asked me the only question I got about what I hoped to accomplish at the NEH. I spoke in generalities, and mentioned again, as I had in my introductory statement, the question of what holds us together as a nation as a possible theme to pursue. It was nice that someone was thinking of the future.

Senator Coats asked me about Jacobowitz talking to me immediately after the incident when I was speaking at Hillel, which

I do not remember, as I have explained above. He also asked about another charge that was being circulated by my critics, that I did not allow the ambassador of South Africa to speak in the early 1980s, even though I let Louis Farrakhan speak. The implication is that I followed a double standard, preventing my ideological enemies from speaking but allowing my ideological allies to speak (assuming erroneously that Louis Farrakhan was my kind of guy).

This charge was typical of the attack being made on me in that there was a slim basis in reality, but the critics were being very loose with the truth. The truth was that soon after I arrived at Penn, while apartheid was in full flower, an organization of conservative students asked the South African ambassador to speak at Penn. Unknown to me, Penn had a policy of requiring sponsoring organizations to pay the costs of security for speakers if those costs were going to be unusual. Faced with this bill, the student organization withdrew their invitation to the ambassador. "As soon as I heard that, I said to myself, and indeed said to the provost, 'This isn't right. We really can't have a policy that lets those who can afford it speak and those who can't afford it not speak.' So we changed the policy right away, and therefore there was a different policy in place—in fact, we changed the policy so that the University paid the security costs for speakers who come to the campus. So there was a policy change between that incident with regard to the ambassador from South Africa and Louis Farrakhan's visit."

Senator Coats then wanted to press me about "diversity," wanting to know whether I included ideological diversity among the kinds of diversity that I valued. At the outset, I did not know where he was going with his questions, however, and that lead to the following exchange:

> Senator Coats: I would be interested in knowing how you define "diversity."
>
> Mr. Hackney: We use the Government categories, Senator.

Senator Coats: Then it is important to know how we define it. [Laughter.] And I can assure you, between now and the time this reaches the floor, I'll find out. [Laughter.]

Mr. Hackney: Equal Opportunity Commission standard forms.

Senator Coats then explained that he brought it up because he was concerned about the fairness of the NEH review process. He made the excellent point that the review process had to include advice from a range of viewpoints. Then he cited a Professor Stanley Fish of Duke who had urged his provost not to appoint members of the National Association of Scholars (NAS), a conservative academic advocacy group, to important academic committees.

Senator Coats: I am wondering if you have any particular opinion about the National Association of Scholars and potential representatives from that organization being appointed to committees of the Endowment for the Humanities.

Mr. Hackney: That would not be a disabling factor in their appointments to the National Endowment for the Humanities so far as my recommendations might go. Some of my best friends are members of the NAS. [Indeed, my mentor, C. Vann Woodward was a member, though my own orientation on academic issues is different.]

Senator Coats: Are you one of their best friends?

Mr. Hackney: That is not yet clear. [The NAS did not endorse me but decided not to oppose me either.]

Senator Coats then explained that he believed that the presumption should favor the President in appointments to federal positions, but "there are some deep wounds and deep feelings regarding Dr. Carol Iannone's denial of a position, not as chairman of the National Endowment for the Humanities, but as a member of the advisory board [National Council on the Humanities]." He then described that incident, citing Iannone's endorsement by a long list of distinguished conservative scholars. I said that I had no personal position on the Iannone nomination, but that I agreed in principle that the National Council would benefit from ideological diversity.

As we were having this discussion, the National Council was a solidly conservative bastion, although mostly a distinguished one. Carol Iannone would have done nothing for its ideological diversity, and would have diluted considerably its intellectual distinction. I can understand why Coats was suspicious of me on this matter; the campaign against Iannone had been led by my sector of the ideological spectrum in the academic establishment, though I was not involved. There are, and should be, members of the general public on the Council who have experience as volunteers in humanities organizations, as well as professionals whose experience is in museums, libraries, state humanities councils, or other kinds of non-academic institutions. I suspect that the Iannone opposition flowed from the fact that she presented an ambiguous profile. She was an adjunct associate professor in the Gallatin Division of NYU. Assuming that there is no quota for undistinguished academics, the only reason she was nominated was that she was close personally and ideologically to the Lynne Cheney circle. Most of her published writing had appeared in *Commentary*, edited by Norman Podhoretz who, along with Irving Kristol, the editor of *The Public Interest* and a frequent contributor to the editorial page of the *WSJ*, was a marquee figure of neo-conservatism. I think the academic opposition to Iannone was surprised when Lynne Cheney converted her into a martyr to political correctness, even though Harvey Mansfield and Michael Malbin, who were just as conservative as Iannone but a lot more distinguished, were approved by the Senate Committee at the same time as Iannone was being turned down.[1]

Naturally, I did not venture these guesses and observations because I did not want to pick a fight. "Ideological rigidity is not me, frankly," I said. "Fairness, I think, is. And I do think that diversity needs to be represented there [on the Council]."

In closing, Harris Wofford emphasized his feeling, which was really his hope, that the Committee would be approaching this nomination in a bipartisan spirit, contrary to the assertion of the *WSJ*. He prompted me to reiterate my position on political correctness, in response to Charles Krauthammer's column, and he raised Jack Danforth's op-ed column as a reply to the Carol Iannone "pay back time" theme. "I have seen you engage in acts of courage over many years," said Harris, "but I am delighted that you have the courage to be a nominee."

After a salute to my wife, and a pointed reference to the fact that she is the niece of Hugo Black, Senator Kennedy closed the hearing: "I intend to ask the committee to move the nomination as soon as possible, and I expect him to be confirmed by a solid bipartisan majority in the United States Senate."

I was thoroughly wrung out. I had been on red alert for just under three hours, and I was more than ready to quit. I walked up to the dais and thanked each Senator for spending so much time on the hearing and for being so fair. In the milling about with the few members of the staff of the NEH who had been there, and the White House contingent, I got the impression that my supporters thought I had done well and that the hearing was a success. The real test of that would be the vote of the Committee, which would take place later.

My gang of family and friends ambled down Capitol Hill and had a celebratory lunch at an excellent French restaurant. I don't remember much about the conversation during the meal, except that it was upbeat. I was close to being comatose, my mind full of doubts and second thoughts. I should have said . . . Why didn't I say . . . It was impossible for me to gauge whether I had changed any minds either among the Senators or among the press. The big thing was that it was over.

During the following week, I was not in Washington because I was moving out of Eisenlohr and out of the president's office in College Hall. I kept in touch with Don Gibson, the acting chairman at the NEH, Martha Chowning, Melanne Verveer and Nestor Davidson. They were all optimistic about the forthcoming vote. The consensus was that I should win the endorsement of the Committee by a 14-3 margin, or perhaps 13-4. Either would be good and would position me well for an anticipated floor fight. It had been a nightmare, and there was more unpleasantness to come, but I finally became confident that I would be confirmed.

On Bastille Day, July 14, I got the call from Martha Chowning, who had been monitoring the situation with Nestor. The Committee had just voted, she reported, and it was unanimous—17-0! Wow, unanimous in favor of confirmation. I was elated.

7

FLOOR FIGHT

O N SUNDAY, JUNE 27, 1993, I sat in the ruins of my study in Eisenlohr, empty shelves staring mournfully at me, amidst the packing crates containing the books that had comforted and instructed me over the past twelve and a half years as president of Penn. It was the first quiet moment I had had all spring in which to absorb the significance of the rude jolt of discontinuity that was about to reroute two lives lived at full pace.

I was still brooding about the hearing. Even though I knew that it had gone very well, I was trapped in a depressed mood, unable yet to get excited about the future into which we were being hurled. This was a familiar condition with me, a kind of "unfocused anxiety," and it comes upon me when things seem to be going well. My experience tells me that every time there is a triumph, there is an unexpected threat not far behind. In this case, I could expect my opposition to start reinterpreting the hearing almost immediately. Perhaps it is the touch of Calvinism that most Protestant Americans—or perhaps most Americans—have somewhere in their core. God is testing us with success, which breeds pride, which causes disaster.

I was feeling very good about what Lucy and I had been able to do at Penn. In his letter in the *Almanac* in April, just after the White

House had announced the President's intention to nominate me, Al Shoemaker had written extravagantly that, "Penn's accomplishments since Sheldon's arrival in February 1981 are without parallel in higher education. He has clearly been one of Penn's greatest chief executives." You will notice, gentle reader, that this differs from the verdict rendered by Alan Kors in chapter three. I much prefer the judgment of my boss and collaborator. Whatever the final assessment of Penn's progress during our tenure, it had been achieved against great difficulties. We had mixed our blood, sweat, and tears with Penn and felt very much a part of it. Leaving, then, was all the more sad.

The evening before, a group of our close Penn friends came for supper. A couple of us trekked around the corner to the Joyful Inn and brought back armloads of Chinese food, spread it out in paper cartons on the elegant dining room table, beneath the portrait of Penn's founder, Benjamin Franklin. We ate and grew prematurely nostalgic.

The movers came the next day. Lucy oversaw the operation. Our things went into storage to await the Senate's decision about our fate, and Lucy drove to our summer house on the Vineyard. That was not a bad place to be while contemplating the uncertainties of unemployment. I went to Fort Worth for the opening of a show of the drawings and models of Penn's great professor of architecture, Louis Kahn. The show was at the Kimball Art Museum, one of Kahn's most delightful buildings. It was my last official act representing Penn.

I got to the Vineyard the following Friday, July 2, and settled in for a wait. I was unemployed, it is true, but not idle. Even though it is against all Washington etiquette, and consequently very bad politics, to appear to be taking Senate confirmation for granted, I began quietly to get involved with affairs at the NEH. Don Gibson was doing well as acting chairman, but he didn't want to do things that would have to be undone once I arrived, so he consulted me.

He was a career civil servant who had been at the NEH since Joe Duffy's chairmanship in the late 1970s. He was trusted by the staff, and I came to trust and rely on him as well. He was not only a historian with good intellectual taste across a broad front of humanities fields, he was a master of getting things to happen without running afoul of the civil service regulations and without being defeated by bureaucratic behavior. We became close allies and good friends.

The August meeting of the National Council on the Humanities was approaching with a full schedule of grant applications to review and decide upon. Since the Council was jam-packed with conservatives who would be very suspicious of me, including my Javert, Alan Kors, I didn't want to make any mistakes the first time out. In addition, the appropriation process was in its busy season on the Hill, and the NEH had $177 million at stake. Beyond these immediate concerns, there were relations with the NEH's various constituencies to worry about. How could we launch a long-term planning process in a way that engaged not only the staff but the state humanities councils and the other humanities groups that were members of the National Humanities Alliance? The NEH was allocated only six political (*i.e.*, non-civil-service) appointments, but they would be crucial to the leadership of the agency. The sooner I could make those, the better. What about the organizational structure itself? Did it suit me? While these interesting problems rattled around in my head, I read John Frohnmayer's cautionary memoir, *Leaving Town Alive*, about his brief interlude as chair of the Mapplethorpe-plagued NEA as well as Michael Straight's biography, *Nancy Hanks*, about the legendary early chairperson of the NEA.

The future began to intrude upon my golf and family time. Thirteen people, including children and grandchildren, were cavorting through our Vineyard house. Every bed was filled, almost every minute as well. All of our usual summer companions were on the island, so social life was hectic but interesting. The party of July was Mike Wallace's 75th birthday party at his house near ours, on a bluff overlooking Vineyard Haven harbor. There were a hundred or so of his closest friends. Art Buchwald was the master of ceremonies. Bill Styron read a very funny piece about Mike's hair still being dark. George Plimpton, a Wallace friend but not usually a Vineyard person, organized a display of fireworks from a barge anchored just off the Wallace beach. Rose Styron and Lucy sang a song to Mike with their own lyrics.

Between family affairs and neighborhood frolics, I talked to Don Gibson and Martha Chowning about the NEH. After much worrying of the question, I decided not to call Richard Cohen about his negative column in the *Washington Post*. Don and Susan Rappaport wrote a letter to the editor correcting Cohen's most blatant error of fact. Nor did I call Meg Greenfield about the *Post*'s editorial. She would undoubtedly say that Amy Schwartz's column on July 1 had set the record straight about what I actually said in my "two-values-in-conflict" statement. Amy's column was mostly about how unedifying the campaign against me was, a "pre-confirmation battle conducted mostly by spitball," but it had the virtue of quoting the part of my statement about free speech being the paramount value in the University.[1]

I got the news about the unanimous committee vote on Wednesday, July 14. My spirits lifted considerably. I was therefore in a good mood as Lucy and I drove with Federal District Judge Mark Wolf and his wife, Lenny, up island to have lunch with their friends from Cambridge, Alan and Carolyn Dershowitz, and their son, Elon. Bob Brustein joined us there. Carolyn is a psychological therapist at a school for "at risk" youth in Boston, so we talked a bit about children, which is Lucy's professional commitment as well. Then the conversation turned, as it was meant to do, to restrictions on government sponsored speech. Alan is very bright, so I enjoyed the conversation, though it was too short and too jumpy to be conclusive. Alan took the position that there should be some criteria for the funding of government sponsored programs other than censorship on the one hand and "anything goes" on the other hand. Bob and I held the line at no restrictions beyond the Supreme Court definition of obscenity. The referee announced "no decision." Alan did suggest that I assemble a group to give me advice about particular questions involving the boundaries of what should be funded with taxpayers' money. That made sense.

I got back to our house from that pleasant excursion about 3 o'clock, and I immediately got on the phone to Kennedy, Wofford, and a host of other people who helped get me to this point. It was fun to be thanking people for a success, even though we still faced a battle on the floor of the Senate.

The next day, I flew to Washington and camped out in Art Buchwald's condo at the Westgate, overlooking Rock Creek Park and the edge of Georgetown. Friday was spent calling on two Senators, having lunch with David Morse from Penn, whose intelligence network in Washington had been a huge help to me, and talking with Melanne Verveer in the First Lady's office about personnel at the NEH. I also dropped in at the NEH and sat in with Don Gibson at a "pre-council" meeting, at which a division's staff presents and discusses the applications that are to be reviewed by the National Council at its next meeting. This is the occasion at which the staff alerts the chairman to any problematic applications. Widely divergent evaluations from peer review panels and outside readers are the most typical problem. This is where the staff really earns its money. They have managed the process. They can usually report not only what particular evaluators said, but frequently they have a sense about why there are differences of opinion. In addition, they have their own opinions about the value of projects. I was impressed at their professionalism that day and never changed my opinion.

The "up" of the committee vote was followed quickly by the

"down" of a "hold" that some anonymous Senator put on my confirmation. Senate rules allow any Senator, without his identity being known publicly, to halt any nomination from going forward. Frequently "holds" are used to pressure the administration into taking some action that a Senator wants, and the action need not be related to the nomination in any way. It is a curious thing. In fact, it is a very bad thing and ought to be changed. I still do not know who held up my nomination from going to the floor of the Senate. It was very frustrating. I recalled that Dr. Everett Koop had preceded me from Penn to Washington. As Surgeon General, he was a huge success, but his confirmation had been held up an unconscionably long time. I took some solace in that.

I stayed in Washington the last ten days of July, trying to round up support, and also trying to get ready for the August meeting of the National Council, on the assumption that I would be confirmed by then. I called on Senator Alan Simpson, the minority whip, in one of the offices in the Capitol used by party leadership. I found him an absolute delight. He was straightforward, a little profane, very funny, and amazingly perceptive. He had been a friend of the NEA and the NEH for some time, and he promised to do what he could to help get my nomination to the floor and get it through. I continue to be a great admirer, though his votes coincided with my opinions only about half the time. One of the great tragedies of the 1990s is that a lot of able moderates of both parties decided to leave Congress, leaders such as Simpson, Nancy Kassebaum, and Bill Bradley.

Harris Wofford told me that Bill Bradley was not terribly enthusiastic about me, so I went to see him. It was such a low-key conversation that I still do not know what to make of it. I think I answered his questions about my record, but he warned me that my big problem was not going to be free speech on campus but would be the scandal then breaking in Louisiana. A nineteenth-century deal between Tulane and the state called for Tulane to provide a certain number of scholarships for Louisiana students, and those scholarships were traditionally awarded by the mayor and individual legislators to students who had been admitted to Tulane. Someone had just noticed that they had been finding their way to the children of important Louisiana politicians and their friends. This is hardly out of character for Louisiana politics, of course, but it worried me because I could not remember anything about it. I assumed that the shenanigans with the scholarships started after I had left and had nothing to do with me—but it would be easy for my enemies to drop hints and raise eyebrows enough to cause me some trouble. Even though I took Bradley's warning seriously, the question was never raised by anyone.

Just as the "hold" on my confirmation appeared mysteriously, it disappeared just as mysteriously, and the Democratic leadership scheduled floor debate for August 2. Without many days left, I did what I could to convert doubters and reinforce supporters.

Full of hope, I arrived at the chairman's office on the fifth floor of 1100 Pennsylvania Avenue, the Old Post Office Building, on Monday morning, August 2. Don Gibson offered to let me watch the Senate proceedings on the office television set. He and other senior staff would be wandering in and out, getting the flavor of the discussion in the gaps between their other tasks.

Before the Senate went into session Nestor Davidson called with ominous news. The Republican leadership, clearly under pressure, wanted "ample time to explore my qualifications" on the floor of the Senate, so a five-hour time limit had been adopted. I would have preferred a perfunctory thirty minutes allocated entirely to supporters. The gargantuan five-hour limit signaled plans for a major trashing. Nestor still felt confident about the outcome, but ugly opposition on the floor would further taint my public image, if that was possible, and a close vote would undercut my perceived authority.

Senator Chafee during the debate pointed out that the dispro-

portionate amount of time the Senate was spending on my confirmation was an indication of how symbolic politics had begun to
push aside substantial and serious matters. Since the "debate" takes
place in a mostly empty Senate chamber, the arguments are aimed
not so much at other Senators, or the staff persons who have been
delegated to monitor the proceedings for their Senator, but at the
C-Span audience. There is a surprisingly large national audience of
C-Span junkies, and there is as well an official Washington audience that watches proceedings with one eye while keeping its other
eye on its other tasks. The major reason, however, for a Senator to
appear in the well to speak on any particular subject is to make a
record, to add a snippet to his public biography, to sculpt himself
for the consumption of his public. Excerpts from the *Congressional
Record* are mailed to voters. Even better, television clips of the
Senator in action are sent to television news programs back home.
It was not about me. I was merely to serve as the foil.

When the order of business reached my nomination, Harris
Wofford took the floor as the manager of this matter for the
majority. He performed brilliantly. He began with a long hymn of
praise for me and my career. I hoped that would go on for the entire
five hours, but he quickly ran out of material. He also entered into
the record a mass of supportive documents: the citation for my
honorary degree from Penn, Senator Danforth's op-ed column
from the *Washington Post*, my statement before the Labor and
Human Resources Committee, the letter of support from Mrs.
Walter H. (Lee) Annenberg, the letter to the Penn community
from Al Shoemaker announcing my intended departure, and
letters from Leonard Lauder, a Penn trustee and head of Estee
Lauder Companies; Sondra Meyers, cultural consultant to the
governor of Pennsylvania; Congressman Joe McDade; William
Luers, President of the Metropolitan Museum of Art; and Mike
Wallace's letter-to-the-editor of the *WSJ*. Harris answered all the
major criticisms of me that had arisen at the hearing or that had

been circulating in the scurrilous press, and he leaned especially heavily on the unanimous vote of the Labor and Human Resources Committee and the broad bipartisan support it indicated.

Senator Jesse Helms of North Carolina was the leading opponent and the first to speak. He began by denouncing political correctness. Then he said, "Mr. Hackney's problem is that he is recognized as one of the most prominent apologists for political correctness." That statement had so little to do with the record of my confirmation hearing, or with the facts about my beliefs and behavior, that it was clear that we were about to witness St. George slaying the dragon of left-wing radicalism for the edification of the folks back home, and perhaps as a way of reminding movement conservatives that they had a champion in the Senate.

I discovered that I could not bear to listen to such a travesty against the truth, even though I understood that it was just political theater. I left the chairman's office and went down the hall to the conference room of the President's Committee on the Arts and Humanities. There I studied grant applications that were going to go before the Council later in the month, and I tried not to think of what was going on eleven blocks away. Later, I read through the *Congressional Record*, a fast, *post facto* experience that is not as traumatic as hearing it in real time.

Senator Helms quoted Charles Krauthammer, criticized me for opposing ROTC on campus, for persecuting Eden Jacobowitz, for forcing Murray Dolfman to undergo sensitivity training, and for defending black students who had stolen the campus newspaper. His presentation of those offenses against humanity never threatened to coincide with the path of truth. Then Senator Helms turned his attention to his real problem with me. I had defended the NEA for funding the Robert Mapplethorpe show, the show that remade Helms's career as a regent of the religious right. My support of a rule prohibiting students from calling each other hateful names became in Helms's telling my support of rules prohibiting students and faculty from speaking freely: "free speech for me but not for thee," he said, expropriating the title of Nat Hentoff's book as well as his blinkered vision.

Something of the agenda of movement conservatism, to neutralize the home base of liberals in academia, is revealed in Helms's assertion that I represent the arrogant academics that Bill Bennett had stood up against when he was chairman of the NEH.

Helms said, "I recall, Madam President, about ten years ago a fellow named Bill Bennett came to Washington to become chairman of the NEH. This was prior to his later becoming Secretary of Education. One of Bill Bennett's great contributions to the NEH was his infusing the agency with the courage to stand up to the smug bureaucrats and their acolytes in academia who, until then, had pretty much dictated who and what was favored in the disbursement of the NEH fund.

"Madam President, the problem is that, once confirmed, Dr. Hackney will undo the good Bill Bennett achieved at the NEH. Dr. Hackney's record gives fair warning that that will be the case, and that is reason enough for this Senate to oppose his nomination."

Helms then circled back and provided more details about the transgressions that he had already cited, quoting from adverse commentators in the press, and inserting into the record the text of the *Washington Times* editorial from that morning that opposed my nomination, as well as some of the *Wall Street Journal* editorials, the Krauthammer column, the Richard Cohen column from the *Washington Post*, and others. Helms ended his remarks by saying that he sincerely hoped that he was wrong about me. "And if I am proved wrong," Helms said, "I will acknowledge it publicly and apologize to Dr. Hackney." I have been listening for my phone to ring and watching my mail, but no message from Senator Helms has yet appeared.

In rebuttal, Harris Wofford pointed out that the Committee

had asked probing questions about all the alleged offenses that his good friend, the distinguished Senator from North Carolina, had alluded to and had found my answers satisfactory. He entered into the record the written questions that Senator Kassebaum had posed to me and that I had answered in writing.[2] Those answers directly contradict the "facts" of the charges that Senator Helms made.

After Senators Pell and Kennedy had spoken in support of me, Harris introduced another string of letters and endorsements, including one from the National Humanities Alliance, the chief lobbyist for a coalition of scholarly groups, the Federation of State Humanities Councils, the American Association of Museums, the American Library Association, and other cultural institutions in the humanities.

Then Senator Joe Lieberman of Connecticut rose in opposition to my nomination. Senator Lieberman was the only Democrat to vote against me, but that is not the reason his opposition disappointed me so bitterly. Having heard from Harris that Lieberman was cool toward me, I called him on the Thursday preceding the Monday floor debate. I said that I understood that he had reservations about my nomination and I would greatly appreciate a chance to come talk to him. I thought I could clear up any doubts that he had. He said that he did not really have time. He was returning to Connecticut the next day and was busy until then. I suggested that I send him a package of materials that he might have a chance to look at over the weekend. He said he would appreciate that. I then said that if he still had doubts, after looking at the material, I would appreciate it if he would call me and give me a chance to respond. He said that would be fine. He never called.

I was aware of another one of those curious coincidences that make the world seem smaller than it is. Joe Lieberman had been the college roommate of Mike Wallace's son. When Mike Wallace volunteered to call Senator Lieberman on my behalf, I couldn't say "yes" fast enough. Mike later reported that he had called and lobbied Lieberman to support me. Lieberman had replied reassuringly that Mike need not worry, a response that Mike interpreted as meaning that Lieberman would not oppose, but that was probably intended to mean that Lieberman knew that I had enough votes for confirmation without his. Not only did Lieberman oppose me with his vote, he made a speech.

Even worse, when he rose on Monday to speak against me, he made it sound as if he and I had had the sort of substantive and lengthy discussion that Senator Coats and Senator Judd Gregg had conducted with me. His words were conventionally artful:

"Madam president, I rise regretfully in opposition to the nomination of Dr. Sheldon Hackney to be chairman of the National Endowment for the Humanities. I do so without pleasure, may I say, because this nominee is, by all accounts, a distinguished scholar and a decent man. Indeed, I spoke to Dr. Hackney recently and found him to be as thoughtful, charming, and well-intentioned as his many supporters promised me he would be."

The false compliments are part of the conventions of Senate debate, so they don't trouble me. The deception involved in pretending that he had talked with me I find appalling. Even though it is a very small thing, I think it is very revealing of character, which is not a compliment. Furthermore, it is a confirmation of Tim Wirth's dour view of Washington theatrics. Lieberman argued against me on the basis of the newspaper theft incident as an assault on free speech, which, of course, it was; but I had not stolen the papers nor defended those who had—except in the fevered imagination of the WSJ and right-wing heresy hunters.

I must say that my suspicion about Lieberman was confirmed later when he joined Lynne Cheney in establishing the vigilante group, the American Council of Trustees and Alumni, whose assault on free speech we examined in chapter one. Nor was I surprised when I noted in the fall of 2001 Lieberman criticizing the Justice Department for prosecuting Zacharia Masaoui, the suspected 9/11 terrorist, in the federal district court in northern Virginia rather than in one of the controversial military tribunals; that is a strange position for a civil libertarian to be taking.

Senator Gorton of Washington also stated his opposition to me on the basis of my being enslaved to political correctness, using the newspaper theft as the prime bit of evidence, but also touching upon the Jacobowitz and Dolfman cases. He inserted into the record a statement from Greg Pavlik, the Penn student columnist, who characterized my administration as one of "intellectual fascism."

Harris responded to these assaults by pointing out that the Committee that had looked most closely at the details of the accusations being used by the Senators from Washington and Connecticut had been satisfied with my explanations and had voted unanimously for my confirmation. He read from the Hearing record to refute the supposed facts being cited by the opposition. Senator Kassebaum then spoke for me and inserted again into the record her written questions and my answers.[3] Howell Heflin also spoke gracefully for me, followed by Jim Jeffords, Republican of Vermont, Senator Leahy, Democrat of Vermont, and Senator Coats, Republican of Indiana. The bipartisanship was evident.

Senator Specter then appeared to speak for me, a triumph of Harris's management of the floor debate. Specter said in a brief statement that even though I had mishandled the two events on the campus in the spring, and even though he thought I was not tough enough for the Washington political environment, he was going to vote for me. Friends like that can give a guy low self-esteem, but I suppose I should be grateful.

Senator Larry Craig of Idaho spoke against me, adopting the rhetorical formula from Shakespeare's *Julius Caesar*—"but Brutus is an honorable man." More remarkable, Craig's case against me was entirely about free speech and my sponsorship of speech codes. Attempting a bit of eloquence, Craig said, "Daily we use words as weapons—and as shields. So I hope my colleagues can also under-stand how words can do more than just express thoughts—they can also shape thoughts." This is not wrong, unless pressed too far, but, ironically, it is a tenet of deconstruction theory, a brand of literary criticism that emphasizes the instability of the meanings of texts, as well as their multiple meanings which can only be under-stood if the texts are unmade or taken apart. Craig would hate it if he understood it, though a deconstructionist would have found a more playful way to put Craig's point, perhaps: "Words don't *express* what we think, they *tell* us what we think. They utter us, rather than the reverse; they conspire with each other to determine who we are." Craig continued:

"But if any of my colleagues are uncertain about the folly and evil of speech codes, let me bring this debate home to you. This is where I have to begin to question the credentials of Dr. Hackney.

"Imagine, for a moment, that we had the same kinds of restrictions in the U.S. Senate that exist on some college campuses today, and that for a time existed at Penn."

That doesn't take much imagination because, in fact, the Senate does have rules of decorum that proscribe disrespectful forms of address! That is just what Penn's racial harassment policy did. Senator Craig then proceeded to misconstrue the nature of Penn's racial harassment policy, pretending that it outlawed any expressions that someone else found offensive. Whatever one thinks of narrowly drawn hate-speech disciplinary rules that are to be enforced through adversarial judicial procedures, and I have said repeatedly that they don't work and ought not to be tried, this description of them is a caricature, a caricature of which the *WSJ* was particularly fond. Craig then makes clear that he is not questioning the regulation of "fighting words," the term the Supreme Court used in the *Chaplinski* case in 1940 to approve limitations on expressions so insulting that they were bound to provoke retaliation. However, Craig missed the point that Penn's racial harassment policy was a very narrowly drawn form of a "fighting words" policy, exactly the sort of regulation that *Chaplinski* permitted.

One could get very huffy about this sort of confusion or misunderstanding in the arguments made by Craig and others. Rather than denouncing it as either dishonest or ignorant, however, we need to see it as an indication that the opposition was not engaged in serious analysis of the Penn policy or of my behavior. It was mounting an attack on an imagined authoritarian Left, a right-wing construct of Leviathan, the political enemy. I doubt that Senator Craig ever made a connection between Penn's racial harassment policy and either the rules of decorum of the Senate or the "fighting words" doctrine. He was going straight ahead against the demon Left. If I happened to be standing in the line of fire, too bad.

My defenders chose not to engage in the hermeneutics of hate-speech bans. They were undoubtedly shrewd in that approach. It proved impossible to correct all the misinformation about the simple facts of the incidents at Penn. It would have been a losing struggle to try to have a reasonable discussion about what we mean when we say we are for free speech. In the political arena, as in much of human thought, binary choices are the rule. It is either this way or that way; I am going to vote either yes or no. It is OK to balance a list of plusses against a list of minuses and conclude that, on balance, choice A is better than choice B. What is not successful is any argument that recognizes that we hold all manner of important but contradictory principles at the same time. We apply those principles differently in different situations—and we are usually not able beforehand to describe all the possible situations in which we would apply principle A rather than principle B or C.

As Poor Richard taught us, we believe that, "He who hesitates is lost." We also believe that one should, "Look before you leap." The trick is to know which of those two conflicting aphorisms we should apply in a given situation.

I am against torture. It is not humane. However, I can imagine resorting to torture in order to extract information about, say, the imminent explosion of a terrorist's bomb in a crowded venue. The lives of many are more important than the pain of a few. I imagine that most Americans would agree with the use of torture in this situation—if the facts are clear and are as I have stated them. Is that example too easy? What if I am not certain that my suspect has the information I need to save lives? How certain do I have to be in order to justify the torture? Can torture be justified for anything other than for the saving of innocent lives? We quickly get into morally ambiguous territory.

All societies prohibit murder, but how is it defined? Killing in self-defense is permitted in some circumstances in the United States. We authorize some members of our society to kill for the common good: soldiers in war; police in life threatening situations. There are various degrees of homicide, depending on such things as intent or premeditation. Exploring such questions in winner-take-all public debates is extremely difficult, especially when the purpose of the debate is not to illuminate the truth but to defeat one's opponent.

In any case, after Craig had finished, the opposition ran out of speakers, bringing the debate to an end after only about three hours. Someone came down the hall to tell me it was safe to come out. The vote was conducted the next day, Tuesday. I watched, fascinated, not knowing what to expect. I was confirmed, 76 to 23. My support was strong and bipartisan.

The Republicans split 22-22. A glance at the tally reveals that Senators generally considered to be moderates tended to support me, while Senators thought of as being further to the right opposed me. Nothing new there. Now, is the difference between the moderates and the conservatives in the Republican party, using this confirmation vote as a rough proxy, a difference between two understandings of free speech? Did the Nays care more for free speech than the Yeas? I think the answer to that question is, no.

There are always a lot of idiosyncratic motivations involved in these votes, of course. For instance, Senator Thurmond supported me. Was that because of Mrs. Annenberg's visit? D'Amato opposed me even though a number of influential Penn alumni in New York lobbied him for me. With a close race coming up, did he need to show his party colors? On the other hand, Lieberman deserted his party. I don't pretend to know why he did that, but it is possible that he saw the events at Penn in the spring of 1993 as another sad chapter in the unlovely history of black-Jewish conflict, and he was showing his solidarity. While I cannot know that that is the case, I am confident that his vote and his speech were not about me or free speech.

Still, in general, the Republican division was along moderate-conservative lines. Those lines do not trace differences on free speech; they demarcate overall orientations to politics. Moderates operate on the pragmatic theory that today's opponent may be tomorrow's supporter, and that to get anything done in Washington, you need to be able to work across party lines. Movement conservatives, however, see the opposition as an enemy to be crushed, heretics whose subversive influence is destroying society and undermining culture. The task is not to get things done piece by piece, but to change the regime, to reorient the thinking and the direction of the country at large. It is not about individual acts of legislation or particular appointments, it is about increasing the influence of "our" way of thinking and decreasing the influence of "their" way of thinking. There is a left wing version of this as well, which liberals like me used to label the "kamikaze left." It would rather lose everything, and maintain its purity, than win a few good things if it required compromising.

After the confirmation vote, Robert Knight, speaking for the Family Research Council, which had lead the opposition to me, said, "I think it was a rather anemic response on the part of the Republicans. . . . we will be paying close attention to his tenure."[4] Others also sounded the theme that I would be watched closely, as I was. I told the *Chronicle of Higher Education* that I was not worried about the heightened scrutiny. "If our criterion for the selection among grant applicants, in the programs we run, in the things we do, in the thought that we stimulate is always one of excellence," I said, against all evidence to the contrary, "then I think we will not go very far wrong."[5]

I was greatly relieved. I called my supporters in the Senate to thank them for shouldering the burden of my confirmation. I also called Lucy who had come to town in anticipation of a victory. We had planned a swearing-in ceremony for the following day, Wednesday, August 4, in the afternoon. Our long-time friend, Federal District Judge Louis Pollak, came down from Philadelphia to administer the oath. The staff of more than two hundred fifty, along with my intrepid confirmation team, gathered in the cavernous assembly room on the first floor of the Old Post Office Building. I introduced my wife and Senator Jeffords (then a Republican of Vermont), who was good enough to attend. I then said a few not very profound things. I referred to the confirmation process as having been rather rough and ugly: "I really don't think you can understand how wonderful it is for me to be here." That brought an outburst of laughter. The mood in the room was joyful. Lou administered the oath, and my career as a government bureaucrat began.

The first set of Council meetings over which I presided went very well. There were no ideological disagreements and the Council members seemed welcoming and pleasant. I thought the staff of the NEH was responding very nicely to me, and I was enjoying being there, at last. As soon as Congress went into its Labor Day recess, I left town like everyone else. Well, not exactly like everyone else. Learning that the Clintons had decided to vacation on Martha's

Vineyard, I hitched a ride up with them on August 19. I have never enjoyed a trip to the Vineyard more.

As Air Force One cruised along on the quick hop to the Vineyard, I told the President how pleased I was finally to be at work at the NEH. The confirmation was a real victory. "Yes," he said, "That is one nomination that we handled right."

EPILOGUE

I SURVIVED AND reached my destination, Washington. The University also survived. In fact, Penn continued to thrive without a downturn in any of the measurable indices of success: applications, admissions, matriculations, fund raising, or rankings. Universities are resilient and have long-cycle metabolisms. People, however, carry scars.

Even though their outer circumstances don't betray it, the young people involved in the water buffalo incident were wounded. I grieve for both Eden Jacobowitz and the black women who were the victims of the verbal assault in which he participated. They all suffered through the long semester of justice denied. I also am sorry for the white students in the high-rise mob who slunk away after their attack. Feelings of remorse must have battled self-justifying rationalizations in their hearts as they watched the tragedy of errors unfold on campus through the spring of 1993. The residue left by this episode on the character of all those who were touched directly by it is impossible to know, but it cannot be good.

For me, telling the story of this little snippet of my life has been a liberating experience in several ways. It has exorcised the subdued sense of anger that has been weighing upon my soul since the events of 1993. In addition, living through that spring and summer was so intensely terrible that I was not aware then of many of the people and events and forces impinging upon my life. I understand what happened much better now.

·Reliving those events as an observer has also made me realize how blessed I was at the time to have so many friends and family members who stood by me. I would not recommend this kind of experience as a way of being awakened to the force-field of love that levitates us even in our darker moments. Most of the Penn trustees and Penn-connected friends had to cross party lines in order to help, proving that the broad center embraces people of good will and good sense of both political persuasions.

Furthermore, I am no longer a character in someone else's drama. I have reclaimed my life, snatched it back from the uncaring hands of authors who were oblivious to me as a whole human being, and who were interested in me only as a puppet who could be made to do a dance in their puppet show.

Lest this sound too much like the death chant of a martyr, let me hasten to add that I was never so encapsulated in my own misery that I thought of myself as a victim. I was not born with a silver spoon in my mouth, but I was not born in a log cabin either. I have long been aware that whatever I did for myself to get to the presidency of Penn and the nomination to be chair of the NEH pales in comparison to the advantages with which I began and the help I got along the way. In fact, as I read back through the text that I have created, it sounds a lot like *People* magazine. No wonder right-wing populists had an easy time using me as a symbol of the eastern elite establishment. I am! No wonder I was eventually able to survive; I have friends in high places!

Apart from the personal therapy that impelled me to take pen to paper, or more accurately to take keyboard to computer, I wanted to document the distortions the new media environment has introduced into public life, the ease and rapidity with which destructive myths can be created and can take on a life of their own.

While at the NEH, I talked often about the threat to our democracy posed by the "drive-by debates" that dominate the public square. I believe my story illustrates how difficult it is for a centrist to operate in an environment that thrives on polarization, and how the complexity of the real world fares poorly in competition with slogans and simplicity. I think my story presents the anatomy of a smear, as well as the dangers of zealotry.

As I have thought about the story that I have told here, I have had a vague sense that I was missing something. I believe I have told it honestly, and I think that I have highlighted the interpretive lessons that the reader ought to take from the text. Still, there was a resonance in the story that I was not identifying. Suddenly, one day as I was editing, it occurred to me that mine was a story of McCarthyism in a new guise. I had not really thought about why the term "political correctness" was so important to the right-wing groups that were attacking me. Why was I dubbed very quickly the "Pope of Political Correctness"? Leaving aside the use of "Pope" as a way of signaling to Protestant fundamentalists that I was the anti-Christ, the focus of my opposition on the term "political correctness" was a bit of a mystery. It was certainly a smear. It had the advantage of charging me with heresy without having to spell out what that heresy actually is. Even Senator Kassebaum asked me to explain it at my confirmation hearing, as she was puzzled.

Now I realize that "political correctness" is the functional equivalent of "commie" or "red" or "fellow traveler." It is meant to end conversation, to brand as unholy the person or the idea to which it is applied. Fortunately, the atmosphere was not as fearful as in the 1950s, and in our post-Cold War world, the label of "political correctness" is not connected to a dangerous external enemy. The charge, however, was intended to have the same effect. Those who used the charge also frequently invoked George Orwell as their patron, further testimony that they understood themselves to be fighting a subversive force in American life. In order to preempt criticism by comparison, they labeled the forces opposing them within the academy "the new McCarthyism," deftly turning the table of tolerance upside down.

There is another large lesson to be derived from the ways in which the Water Buffalo incident and the newspaper theft were reported, a lesson about politics and public discourse in the United States. We Americans find it very difficult to use the political process to argue directly about values. Indeed, one major strand of American political thought, sometimes called "process liberalism," holds that the government ought not to have anything to do with values. Those are to be left to individuals to choose for themselves. The government should have as little as possible to do with substantive choices about the good life. Another good reason for process liberalism, of course, is that we all believe in a lot of contradictory values at the same time. What we argue about, then, is which of our shared values is applicable in a particular situation. The struggle is about how to frame the issue.

In the great 1981 film directed by Sidney Lumet, *Prince of the City*, the hero is a cop who engages in petty graft along with his buddies on the force. In their world, it was accepted behavior. The Justice Department launches an investigation, and eventually our hero agrees to testify about police corruption. For this, he suffers the psychological torment of the damned. He has violated traditional society's primary value of being loyal to one's family, friends, and clan. At the same time, he has bravely followed modern society's expectation that we all observe abstract rules of behavior thought to be universal, such as honesty and carrying out one's oath of office. Two values that we ordinarily maintain in equilibrium are brought into conflict by this particular situation. The hero is forced to choose between them and is crushed. He is shunned by his former friends, almost murdered by the Mafia, then cast aside by the ambitious federal authorities when he has outgrown his usefulness. It is not so much a cynical tale as an exploration of the cruel ambivalence of values in conflict.

America committed itself at the outset in the Declaration of Independence to both freedom and equality, lofty values that still lie at the core of the American identity. Their meanings have always been ambiguous, and those meanings have changed from time to time and from situation to situation, but they are deeply embedded in the American mind.

A major theme of American history is the varying relationship between freedom and equality as guiding stars of American actions. They do not always pull in the same direction, and we struggle to avoid having to choose between them. One of the flex points in our history, and in the history of our understanding of freedom, occurred in the early twentieth century when it had become clear to progressive reformers that the most important threat to freedom was not the government but private aggregations of power, especially by corporations.

In *The Promise of American Life*, Herbert Croly in 1909 outlined the progressive project for the twentieth century: the use of government as a balance wheel of social justice, to compensate for the fact that the individual in modern, highly specialized and interdependent economies could not be self-sufficient in the sense understood in the old agricultural societies, and was unequal to the organized power of business. The role of government has subsequently been the primary question for American politics in the twentieth century.

Conservatives and liberals typically argue with each other about the role of government by invoking the values of either freedom or equality (understood as equal opportunity). They don't argue about whether equal opportunity is a good thing. Almost all Americans believe it is, and they overlook the fact that Bill Gates's children are going to be more equal than other children, because we also believe that parents ought to be able to give their children whatever advantages they can afford. Conservatives and liberals therefore argue about whether equal opportunity is actually available at any particular historical moment.

Conservatives generally think enough opportunity is available, that the existing distribution of wealth is very close to the existing distribution of merit, and that in any case the free market will work better than the government in the long run. Liberals point to imperfections and obstructions in the availability of opportunity and urge that the government be used to distribute opportunity more equally and to enable individuals to fulfill their God-given potential.

Lately, conservatives have been getting the better of that argument, in part by dramatizing real or imagined fraudulent claims that the less well-to-do make on society's sympathy and charity. The image of "welfare queens" arriving to pick up their government checks in Cadillacs is part of this argument. The public has also been aware of persistent and growing social pathologies despite or because of governmental attempts to abolish poverty and relieve suffering. This has helped reverse the tide of liberalism that washed over the nation from the New Deal through the presidency of Lyndon Johnson.

The Civil Rights Movement of the 1960s was successful because it was able to invoke values that were already deeply embedded in American beliefs, especially equal opportunity and equality before the law. The movement dramatized—literally— the absence of equal treatment for African Americans through sit-ins and freedom rides. Americans saw nine exemplary school children in Little Rock turned back by National Guard troops from the door of Central High School, the symbol of opportunity.

We saw blacks attacked by police dogs and knocked down by high-powered fire hoses in Birmingham. We learned of civil rights workers murdered with the help of local law enforcement officers in Mississippi. These dramas of injustice brought to the surface of the public's consciousness the correctness of the claims of the Civil

Rights Movement. The Movement began to fade and fragment when it became radicalized, when it began to call upon the public to accept new values, such as black nationalism tinged with socialism.

The power of the civil rights text about equality of opportunity put conservatives on the defensive. Barry Goldwater's rout in the 1964 presidential race was in part testimony to the extent to which the narrative of equal opportunity was unchallenged at that time. Conservatism has had a hard time finding a rhetoric that could compete. Eventually, however, Americans grew tired of the claims of minority groups and came to the convenient conclusion that the problems of race had been mostly solved.

At the same time, conservatives began to refashion a narrative about freedom that stood as an alternative to the equal opportunity that was the goal of the Left of the 1960s. Political Correctness was a shorthand slogan in that developing narrative of freedom. It was built in part on the rising resentment against the claims of minority groups for special treatment to allow them to compete equally. This conservative narrative of freedom has overcome the narrative of equality.

So, it is possible to understand the story of my life during the year 1992-93 as being caught up in the competition between two dueling narrative texts: freedom versus equality. Americans believe in both. The trick for my opponents, therefore, was to tell a story of contemporary politics so that freedom became the applicable or threatened value—not equality. Alexis de Tocqueville was wrong, Americans don't prefer equality. They will choose freedom every time. I was confirmed as chair of the NEH because I was able to slip out of "their" story about me and become a real person struggling in a world full of moral ambiguity. I was able to do that only in the personalized, face-to-face arena of the United States Senate.

In the simplified symbol-manipulating world of the mass media, however, enshrined in fuzzy memories, newspaper morgues, and electronic data bases, I am probably still the "Pope of Political Correctness." We must find a way to bring both civility and the moral complexity of the real world into the national conversation that operates through the mass media.

Furthermore, for those who, like me, are committed to social justice in an inclusive society, the task is to devise a politics that links freedom and equality not as binary choices but as mutually reinforcing values in our quest for a more perfect union.

Appendix 1

Higher Education

as a Medium for Culture

The Public Representation of Culture and History
Center for Advanced Study in the Behavioral Sciences
April 16-18, 1998
Remarks of Sheldon Hackney

Whatever one thinks of postmodernism,[1] it has focused our attention on the paradox of free will: we are all at the same time products of our culture and also authors of that culture. We are trapped within our particular context of time and place, within the imposed meanings of our race, class, gender, and other given traits; yet that cultural prison is constantly being renovated, continuously transformed by human thought and action. The lenses through which we perceive the world and ourselves are the products of our own manufacture. We are thus simultaneously subjects and objects of culture.

   The university is caught in the same paradox; it both shapes and reflects the culture within which it is embedded. It is profoundly conservative in that it is the guardian of the accumulated store of human knowledge; it is profoundly radical because it is the

institutionalized instigator of cultural change. The university processes students so as to fit them for service in society as it is, but it
also rips those same students out of their comfortable cultural
moorings and equips them to choose their own values and their
own identities.

Despite this ambiguity, education in American culture has
always borne a great burden. The nation turns to education to solve
seemingly intractable problems. What are we going to do about all
those returning soldiers and sailors after World War II? Let's send
them to college on the GI Bill and let them reenter the workforce
gradually. The Soviet Union launches Sputnik? Let's jack up
education and pour money into university-based research. Are we
developing an urban underclass that seems to live by the mirror
image of mainstream values? Let's reform urban schools.

From the first, education has played an unusually important
role in American life. It was valued in this overwhelmingly Protestant country because it provided access to the word of God. All of
the colonial colleges were church related, with the sole exception of
the College of Philadelphia (now the University of Pennsylvania),
and even it had a clergyman as its first head. Preparation of the
clergy was a central task of these colleges. In addition, the sons of
the elite and the aspiring elite could have their character shaped and
their minds improved by the mental calisthenics that the classical
curriculum was intended to provide.

It is remarkable to realize that at the time of the Revolution,
the population of the thirteen colonies, on the provincial outskirts
of European civilization, was the most literate in the world. Those
reading rates soared after the Revolution, rising from 75 percent to
95 percent in the North between 1800 and 1840—and this was
accomplished before the public school movement had had much of
an impact![2]

For America's radical experiment in popular government,
education has been expected to provide an informed citizenry and

leaders of wisdom and virtue; for a nation of immigrants, and a nation that is highly mobile—even rootless—it is meant to supply the common currency of values and history that holds a diverse nation together; for an economy based on high technology that operates in a global marketplace, it is providing the new ideas and knowledge workers that produce a high standard of living; for a nation that believes in equal opportunity, education is expected to overcome the disadvantages of poverty and discrimination. Expectations are very high!

There is an irony in this, of course, because one of the most powerful strands in the complex American identity is anti-intellectual. In this strand, we understand ourselves as an exceptional nation created by ordinary people seeking a fresh start and a second chance, an escape from the corruptions and oppressions of European civilization, freedom from the dead hand of the past. In this view, we are a people whose moral compass is calibrated by its closeness to nature and its distance from books, a people renewed by the frontier, unconfined by institutions, made special by the constant effort to perfect ourselves—even continuously to remake ourselves individually and collectively. Nevertheless, education has been highly valued.

Higher education in the United States is now the envy of the world. As an export industry, it earns a significant amount of foreign exchange. It also earns what Joe Nye has called "soft power," the admiration of our cultural strength that smooths the way for American diplomats in dealing with other countries and other cultures. Public opinion polls indicate that higher education has managed to maintain the confidence of the public even during the three-decade decline of confidence in all institutions of American life. Even in the grubby terms of economics, higher education is calculated to be a good investment for individuals and for society as a whole. The gap between what a college graduate earns at age thirty and what a high school graduate earns at age thirty is wide and getting wider. The positive correlation between a society's education levels and economic development is strong and getting stronger.

Unfortunately, the university is strategically situated in American culture. Any movement interested in shifting cultural values one way or another may view higher education as the high ground that must be seized or at least neutralized. One can already hear policy analysts, pundits and legislators saying, in effect, education is too important to leave to the educators. When the public begins to look at colleges and universities, as it is beginning to do, what it will see are institutions whose internal cultures are very different from other institutions in society. Tenure is difficult to understand in a world of increasing job insecurity. Shared governance is difficult to explain to a world that values efficiency and responsiveness, whose fondest cliché these days is "lean and mean." The absence of price competition in large sectors of higher education is hard to accept by a public addicted to K-Marts and hyperstores. For a public habituated to mergers followed by a massive amputation of jobs, the absence of such activity in higher education will seem strange. Why, furthermore, is it not possible to apply the wonders of information technology in wholesale ways to deliver an educational product that is both high quality and inexpensive?

The more the public looks, the more higher education is going to seem to be a candidate for "reinventing." Universities thus face the possibility of catastrophe by inadvertence, damage by trustees or legislators who see the university as a knowledge factory, as Clark Kerr described it in 1963 in the Godkin Lectures, and try to manage it accordingly.[3]

A more direct and real threat stems from the university's reluctant role as a major actor in the Culture Wars. The term "actor" is appropriate because the Culture Wars are a kind of theater, a theater in which the contenders plot scenes and follow scripts designed to send cultural messages. The purpose is to harness the university to the task of pulling the culture in a particular direction.

The culture,[4] of course, is constantly in motion, pushed and pulled this way and that by innumerable influences, some of them large and impersonal, such as changing technology, some of them quite self-conscious. For example, the extraordinarily successful women's movement, since its rebirth with Betty Friedan's *Feminine Mystique* in 1963, proceeded along two fronts at once.[5] One front was public policy. It advocated new laws designed to prevent discrimination against women in hiring and in pay, and that were intended to protect women from harassment in the workplace. The notion was that laws would change behavior and behavior would change the culture.

At the same time, however, the movement assaulted the patriarchal biases in the culture directly by attacking the language in which those biases were encoded, and by confronting the manners that were the reflection of the cultural biases. It seemed silly to have to use gender-equal "him/her" rather than the privileged "him," and it was a nuisance to learn to use the neutral salutation "Ms." in order to avoid the culturally loaded "Miss" or "Mrs.," but those tactics had the desired consciousness-raising effects. Behaving as if "the personal is the political" struck many as bad manners, but it worked. The culture changed in the intended direction.

The religious right is following a course similar to the women's movement by seeking to capture the government for some of its purposes (prevention of abortion; teaching creationism in school; protecting prayer in schools; character education; etc.), and by waging at the same time cultural warfare in the public square over powerful symbols (prayer at public events; the invocation of religiously derived values in public policy debates; respect for the flag; recitation of the pledge of allegiance; etc.).

The counterculture of the 1960s, on the other hand, did not

trust the government, and disdained the political movements of the 1960s as well. It simply ran a large-scale cultural demonstration project by turning almost every middle-class virtue upside down, and then singing and living the new lifestyle. "Let your culture be your politics," they said, and bombarded the public with a long string of slogans: "do your own thing," "if it feels good, do it," "never trust anyone over thirty," "tune in, turn on, and drop out," "make love, not war," etc.

We should not be surprised, therefore, when the counterrevolutionaries of the current Culture Wars focus upon universities, dedicated as those cultural warriors are to rolling back the cultural changes initiated in the 1960s by feminism, the Civil Rights Movement, the other social justice movements, the anti-war movement, and the counterculture. The revolutionary army seemed to be bivouaced on college campuses in those turbulent years, and universities are suspected of harboring fugitives from the Sixties.

A steady stream of intellectual criticism has been directed at higher education of late. It began, perhaps, with Secretary of Education William Bennett's high profile attacks on Stanford's curriculum and the intellectual corruption of the academy in general, but continued with a long series of polemical tracts: Allan Bloom's surprise best-seller of 1987, *The Closing of the American Mind: How Higher Education Has Failed Democracy and Impoverished the Souls of Today's Students*; which was followed by Roger Kimball's *Tenured Radicals: How Politics Has Corrupted Our Higher Education*; Dinesh D'Sousa's *Illiberal Education: The Politics of Race and Sex on Campus*; Richard Bernstein's *Dictatorship of Virtue: How the Battle of Multiculturalism Is Reshaping Our Schools, Our Country, Our Lives*; Lynne Cheney's *Telling the Truth: Why Our Culture and Our Country Have Stopped Making Sense and What We Can Do About It;* and more recently by Alan Kors and Harvey Silverglate, *The Shadow University: The Betrayal of Liberty on America's Campuses.*[6]

The collective theme of these books is that intellectual anarchy reigns in higher education; there is no agreement about what an educated person should know. College campuses have capitulated to postmodernism so that there are no fixed meanings anymore, and certainly nothing bearing the name of Truth. Every statement is taken to be a political statement, and the meaning of every text is dependent on the context of the author and the reader. The canon of the Great Western Tradition has been fatally adulterated with "politically correct" respresentives of every currently fashionable victim group. Moreover, this argument continues, objective standards and rationality have been replaced as tests of truth by other political agendas of the Left. As if all of this were not bad enough, cultural storm troopers are imposing a "politically correct" orthodoxy on campuses and stamping out the free speech rights of those who disagree. In summary, the public is being told through an orchestrated vocabulary that a "cultural elite" is undermining traditional values on which our culture depends.[7]

All of the issues seized upon by the critics were in active contention on campuses in the 1980s and 1990s; they are not simply the inventions of demented imaginations. The great deception resides in the assertion that particular universities or all of higher education are dominated by postmodernists, poststructuralists, deconstructionists, critical theorists, black separatists, radical feminists, Marxists, or other allies of Darth Vader. That is just not true. What is especially distressing in the writings of the conservative critics is the absence of any recognition that postmodernism is not an all or nothing proposition. One can benefit from the insights of the new theories without being captured by them. "Cognizant but not coopted" would describe ninety percent of that relatively small number of scholars in the few fields in which the new theories have been active who have even paid enough attention to understand postmodernism. The result is that, instead of an honest argument about why the various new theories are or are not true, we get the polemics of Chicken Little.

Fortunately, this right-wing caricature of higher education does not dominate popular attitudes yet, nor has a broader array of critics been completely successful in convincing the public that faculty are lazy and arrogant, that they pay little attention to undergraduate education, that they spend their days learning more and more about less and less, and that they then report their findings in abstruse jargon that can only be understood by half a dozen specialists around the world, but you can find those stereotypes in a lot of mainstream reportage. The narrative that has cast the university in the role of a cultural Pol Pot has thus already been created. It exists, and it is waiting, dormant in the public mind, to be activated by one incident or another. This semi-coordinated attack is designed, as Robert Hughes has observed in *Time* magazine, "to defoliate the liberal habitat."[8]

The liberal habitat is ground zero in the Culture Wars, and that habitat is on college campuses. After the ideological agent orange has done its work, what then? Well, the university is a cultural prize of considerable import. Whoever can determine and control the cultural message that is represented by the university, and that is transmitted by the university to succeeding generations of students, will gain an immense purchase on the culture itself. So, what does the university mean now? This calls for a little history.

The grand narrative of modernity, evolving out of the scientific revolution of the sixteenth and seventeenth centuries, gradually entranced the Judeo-Christian West with the humanistic notion that the world is completely knowable through the application of human rationality and the scientific method, and that material and moral progress would be the certain results of scientific rationalism. As the grand narrative unfolded in succeeding centuries, the importance of individualism and of free inquiry became attached to the modernist dogma.

In the nineteenth century, universities increasingly absorbed the modernist ideology, paralleling the conversion of society at large. They embraced universalistic values, such as the legitimacy of meritocracy, the necessity of objective tests for truth, the centrality of free inquiry linked to professional standards of intellectual honesty. Those values characterized the modern research univeristy as it developed in the late nineteenth and the early twentieth centuries. It is important, however, to realize that as this new scientific ethos took hold of universities, the older orientations were not completely abandoned.

Recall that colonial and early nineteenth century colleges were devoted to character development and mental conditioning. In addition, after the Revolution, all educational institutions began to pay attention to education for citizenship. That, for instance, was a prominently stated purpose of Mr. Jefferson's university in Charlottesville. As democracy flowered, it became abundantly obvious that American society was not going to be controlled by a single elite that could be prepared by a small number of similar colleges with narrow functional focuses. Colleges and universities began to differentiate and to feature professional education and practical training, "how to earn a living rather than how to live." Emblematic of this relatively new expectation of higher education was the Morrill Act of 1862 which initiated the system of land-grant universities that devote part of their energies to the scientific improvement of agriculture and rural life. Educational pragmatism of this kind remains a distinctive feature of American higher education. The important point for present purposes is that the earlier functions of higher education did not disappear as scientific rationality gradually seized universities in the late nineteenth century. Character building and mental conditioning and preparation for democratic citizenship and instrumental preparation for business and the professions remained among the purposes of increasingly complex institutions.

Nor was the hegemony of science uncontested. The major

counterclaiment for functional primacy in the emerging research university was the "culture movement."[9] Culture in this sense was originally defined by Thomas Carlyle as comprising that part of life that did not have to do with the business of the society. It was championed in the next generation by Mathew Arnold as the study of "the best which has been thought and said." The culture movement dissented from the imperial claims of science and portrayed humanists as the real heart of the university, a secular clerisy that could instruct society on the finer things of life and of the mind. The advocates of the culture movement were formidable, though their rhetoric was laced with elitist assumptions that doomed their effort to capture an institution so important to a democracy.

The culture movement failed to win control of the university, but it did not die out. It persists. We can hear it speaking to us through the voices of Allan Bloom and Lynne Cheney. Theirs is a nostalgia for a golden age that never existed.[10] The winner, of course, in that cultural tussle of the late nineteenth century was scientific rationalism. It has been, and continues to be, regnant, though the vestiges of the competing orientations make for lively debates on campus and off.

The public has come to associate the idea of progress with this self-representation of universities as institutions devoted to the disinterested pursuit of truth and human wellbeing through the preservation, transmission, and creation of knowledge. Universities, in their devotion to cognitive rationality, thus signify the culture of modernity. This is a tremendously important cultural role in contemporary America.

Now, modernity and its patrons have simultaneously come under attack from two directions. The rear is harassed by a revitalization movement feeding upon cultural and religious elements that have never completely accepted the hegemony of science, and that have resisted the seemingly inevitable drift of culture toward materialism and relativistic morality. Pat Robertson and Jerry Falwell would never attack science directly, but they make it clear that when the claims of faith and those of science clash, faith is superior.

Believing in neither faith nor science, postmodernists attack modernity from the front, calling into question any claim by science to objectivity or universality. How can we know what values are universal, they ask, when we are bound so tightly to our own particular cultural contexts, conditioned by our race, class, gender, historical time and place, and personal experience. Try as we might, we cannot get outside of history to look at human experience from some transcendent vantage point. Furthermore, argue the deconstructionists, we are creatures of language. Almost everything we experience is mediated through language, and we know that language is metaphorical, ambiguous and culturally coded. What I think I mean from within my own context by a particular set of words will not be understood by others in their contexts in the same way. Meanings are not fixed. They are especially slippery and malleable when we attempt to transmit them to others. David Lodge, in his wonderfully comic academic novel has one of his characters coin the deconstructionist maxim, "Every decoding is another encoding." [11] This conjures up an endless closed loop of non-communication.

At the extreme, the postmodern stance yields a world in which everyone is the "radical other" in relationship to everyone else. There is no common ground because we are all trapped within our subjective cocoons. It is an incommensurable world with no shared meanings or values. The scientific method is not sacred. Science merely consists of the tests for truth that a particular set of scholars or scientists agree to at any one time. In that kind of world, the university is a futile institution because scholars cannot accurately communicate with each other, much less with students, so truth is relative, more responsive to the ideological needs of a particular set of interests than to any disinterested standards.[12]

At the more optimistic end of the spectrum, however, where almost all scholars live, though we may never arrive at ultimate or universal truths, we can subject truth claims to tests of evidence and the rules of human reason, tests that are likely to get us closer to the truth in our never-ending quest to improve the human condition and increase the store of human knowledge. No answer is absolute or universal, but some answers are better than others, and we can know which those are. Even socially constructed concepts, such as race or class, have some basis in the observable world, some reference to real experience.

It would, of course, be disasterous if a university, or if higher education in general, were to be captured by the extreme postmodern position. Ironically, however, for the university to be true to its cultural identity, it must remain open to postmodernists, and it must face postmodern arguments on their scientifically rational merits. Universities not only profess or teach about values, they "represent" important values. Thus they cannot avoid being "sites of contestation," a built-in source of conflict made even more volatile by the fact that universities organized around multiple and conflicting functions. The arguments get to be so ferocious because there is no real agreement on the criteria that should be applied.

A little-noticed threat to the university is the market place itself. I do not only mean the dangers that lurk in the efforts of universities to benefit from the revenue streams generated by the new ideas created on campus by faculty. The siren song of technology transfer masks real dangers, but those dangers can be avoided by careful thought. A more interesting problem flows from the steady elision of the boundary between the university and the materialistic, individualistic, pragmatic and short-term world of commerce. The culture of the market place is telling young people in particular that they *are* what they *consume*. As we are set increasingly adrift by contemporary life, we feel a heightened need for a clear identity. We are told that we can buy an identity at the shopping center, and we can change that identity frequently. We can continuously repackage ourselves. That this is a delusion makes it no less real. The university, as much as the church, is thus in competition with the market as the place where one determines one's identity. It takes study at the university; it only takes money at the mall. Over the long run, this creates a pressure to see the university in instrumental terms. It is the place where one goes to learn how to make the money that one can then take into the market and buy the accoutrements that make one a particular kind of person. One can only hope that authenticity will continue to have some value in the identity markets of the future.

Universities are thus beset by potential problems having to do with their cultural identity and their function as a medium that transmits cultural values in multiple ways. Conflict cannot be avoided, but what should universities do to preserve their value? First, they should avoid taking institutional positions on matters that do not have to do with their core values or immediate institutional interests. It will be expected that universities vehemently insist on there being no outside constraints on free inquiry and open expression. That must be done.

Even so, conflict will occur. It will arise from the value content of the practical activities the institution must pursue in order to function in the real world. It must hire and fire faculty (according to what standard?); it must admit students (and how representative of the population should they be?); it must house and feed and entertain and provide health care for its members (what principles will inform those activities?). Does the university have a chaplain? What faith should she be from? Does the university observe religious holidays? Whose? In all such instrumental activities, what values will the university put into action? Those value choices, and even the process by which those decisions are made, also constitute the meaning of the university's cultural message. Controversy is difficult to avoid.

It would also help if each faculty were self-consciously clear about the standards of professional behavior that it expects its members to follow. In addition each institution should work to knit itself into the fabric of its communities, both local and national, so as to be seen as a good neighbor rather than an arrogant and distant mystery when one crisis or another happens to bring the university to public notice. Universities must work harder at telling the story of higher education to the general public.

Interestingly enough, it may help in telling that story to retain, protect and emphasize the mystique that is associated with being so different. Distinctive rituals help communicate the special character of universities. The fuzzy focus that derives from the multiple functions may be as important as the prestige connected to being at the same time the protector of tradition and the voice of modernity. As long as conflict is unavoidable, make the most of the causes of the conflict.

It is comforting to note that the American system of higher education is a reflection of the culture in another important way. Taken as a whole, it is highly competitive among institutions, market oriented with regard to its functions, segmented as to those markets, highly decentralized, geographically and organizationally dispersed so that there are multiple sources of power and authority, meritocratic, and also organized so that there are numerous "second chances" for potential students. A higher percentage of the American population participates in higher education than in any other society, making it more equalitarian, as befits a country whose self-perception is grounded in democracy, and whose shared values importantly include equal economic opportunity and the cultural commandment to perfect oneself and one's community. Even in its structure, the higher education system signals the featured values of American culture.

The promise of an education in the liberal arts is rooted in the twin paradoxes with which we began: by learning about the past, and about the various "ways in which the world works," we gain the power to change ourselves, to liberate ourselves from the benevolent and malevolent shackles of community and tradition. This promise is especially consonant with American culture. The "pursuit of happiness," one of the unalienable rights that the Declaration of Independence identifies as something governments are instituted in order to secure for citizens, meant the freedom to develop one's own capacities, to improve oneself and one's station in life, even to choose one's own identity.

It is true, of course, that no one starts his life of choosing unencumbered by outside influences. We are all situated within a particular cultural context. Our choices are shaped for us. Especially is this true of the least well-off among us. Education can set us free, however. It can give us the power not only to be who we want to be, but to imagine all the kinds of person we might want to be. My own American belief is that our individual fates are linked together in that quest and that ultimately we cannot be who we want to be unless others in our society have the same power. Whatever one's notion of a just society and a life worth living, education plays a critical role. For that reason, education is freighted with cultural significance.

Higher education is the differential gear that links the opposing terms of the paradox of free will, that we are at the same time the subjects and the objects of our culture. American culture is an eclectic system of thought that depends very heavily on the interaction of apparently opposed concepts and bodies of theory and values. In this way we can benefit from the complementary attributes of classical liberal and classical republican ideas, from the mutually reinforcing relationship between our respect for individualism and our love of community, and from the simultaneous pursuit of individual liberty AND equality. Similarly, the American university can find strength in the very multiplicity and ambiguity of its purposes. Sometime it is not so bad to speak with forked tongue.

Appendix 2

Education and the American Identity

Remarks of Sheldon Hackney
National Conference on The Boyer Legacy—Prospects for a New Century
Sponsored by the Boyer Center for Advanced Studies at Messiah College
June 4-6, 1998

From the first, education has played an unusually important role in American life. Preparation of the clergy was a critical task in the colonies, so it is not surprising that all of the nine colonial colleges were church related, with the sole exception of my own, and even the College of Philadelphia had a clergyman as its first head. Aspiring gentlemen, of course, could also acquire appropriate cultural polish, but that was an incidental bit of profane reality. More broadly, education was valued in this overwhelmingly Protestant country because it provided access to the word of God. Even though our colonial forebears lived in stratified, deferential communities, they had been largely lured to these distant shores by the prospect of a better life and the opportunity to improve their station in life. One of the marks of genteel status in the eighteenth century was participation in public life, and for that a little learning was helpful.

It is remarkable that at the time of the Revolution, the

population of the thirteen colonies, on the provincial outskirts of European civilization, was probably the most literate in the world. Those reading rates soared after the Revolution, rising from 75 percent to 95 percent in the North between 1800 and 1840—and this was accomplished before the public school movement had had much of an impact! (The South lagged among the white population and consciously repressed literacy among slaves.)

After the Revolution, of course, education for citizenship became a tune anxiously whistled into the winds of doubt about the viability of democracy. For our radical experiment in self rule, education has been expected to provide an informed citizenry and leaders of wisdom and virtue; for a nation of immigrants that is also highly mobile—even rootless—it is meant to supply the common currency of values and history that holds a diverse nation together; for an economy based on high technology, operating in a global marketplace, it is providing the new ideas and knowledge workers that produce a high standard of living; for a nation that believes in equal opportunity, education is expected to overcome the disadvantages of poverty and discrimination.

Indeed, the nation seems to turn to education to solve every daunting problem. What are we going to do about all those returning soldiers and sailors after World War II? Let's send them to college on the GI Bill so that they won't flood the job market. The Soviet Union launches Sputnik? Let's jack up education and pour money into university-based research. American businesses having trouble competing in the new global economy? We must reverse "the rising tide of mediocrity" in our schools in order to save "A Nation at Risk." Are we developing an urban underclass, an oppositional culture that lives by a mirror image of mainstream values? We must reform urban schools. Education bears a heavy burden in American culture!

There is an irony in this, of course, because anti-intellectualism frequently appears as a feature of one of the most powerful strands in the complex American identity. In this strand, we understand ourselves as an exceptional nation created by ordinary people, people seeking a fresh start and a second chance, an escape from the corruptions and oppressions of European civilization, freedom from the dead hand of the past, made special by the constant effort to perfect ourselves—even continuously to remake ourselves individually and collectively. There is a pastoral version of this view that sees us as a people whose moral compass is calibrated by its closeness to nature and its distance from books, a people renewed by the frontier, unconfined by institutions, drawing wisdom and virtue directly from human nature untainted by the artificiality of "book learning." Nevertheless, the respect for knowledge and therefore for education has been more central in our identity.

There are other ironies. Higher education in the United States is now the envy of the world. As an export industry, it earns a significant amount of foreign exchange. It also earns what Joe Nye has called "soft power," the admiration of cultural leadership that smooths the way for American diplomats in dealing with other countries and other cultures. Public opinion polls indicate that higher education has managed to maintain a relatively high level of public confidence during the three-decade decline of confidence in all institutions of American life. Even in the grubby terms of economics, higher education is calculated to be a good investment for individuals and for society as a whole. The gap between what a college graduate earns at age thirty and what a high school graduate earns at age thirty is wide and getting wider. The positive correlation between a society's education levels and economic development is strong and getting stronger. So, why am I so worried?

I believe it may be because I expect that all this success, and the growing importance of higher education in a knowledge-based society, will bring heightened scrutiny. One can already hear policy analysts, pundits and legislators saying, in effect, education is too important to leave to the educators. Surely, you say, higher education is strong enough to withstand honest scrutiny.

Perhaps, but when the public begins to look at colleges and universities, as it is beginning to do, what it will see are institutions that are anomalous in our society. Tenure is difficult to understand in a world of increasing job insecurity, in a society whose fondest cliché these days is "lean and mean." Shared governance is difficult to explain to a world that values efficiency and responsiveness. The absence of price competition in large sectors of higher education is hard to accept by a public addicted to K-Marts and hyperstores. A trustee who has just "right-sized" his company by eliminating a third of the jobs and the people who filled them will wonder why that is not possible in his university, whether or not it needs it. The more the public looks, the more higher education is going to seem to be a candidate for "reinventing."

Now, there are rational explanations for all of these deviant features, but I worry that we are so much governed these days by the sound-byte ethos of the mass media, we will never be able to explain adequately or to reframe the image that has been created by the first superficial characterization. This worries me because, while I think higher education needs to change in various ways quite rapidly, I do not think that the needed change is likely to be properly prescribed by outside pressures, be they cost-conscious legislative authorities, bottom-line obsessed business groups, public opinion mobilized by a scandal-mongering press, or ideologically motivated pressure groups.

As one smidgen of evidence, I offer the university's reluctant role as a major actor in the Culture Wars. I use the term "actor" deliberately, because the Culture Wars are a kind of theater, a theater in which the players plot scenes and follow scripts designed to convince an audience that their side is the hero and the other side is the villain. Just as we spoke of the European Theater and the Pacific Theater and the North African Theater in World War II, we now have the *campus theater* in the Culture Wars.

Politics is still about tax codes, the regulation of commerce, and how many tax dollars are going to be spent for what purposes in whose district, of course. Some large and real issues have been occupying politicians recently: health care reform, campaign finance reform, restructuring social security, and balancing the federal budget. Still, to an unusual degree, the public arena lately has been full of arguments about such things as the Enola Gay exhibit at the Smithsonian, school prayer, abortion rights, school vouchers, gays in the military, whether Murphy Brown is a good role model, whether Sister Soulja should be encouraging deviant behavior among young black men, the Mapplethorp exhibit and the pros and cons of Karen Finley as a performance artist. In short, arguments about values-in-conflict have been preempting the politics of resource allocation.

In these Culture Wars, the NEH and the NEA serve as surrogate symbols of modernist culture, a culture that is thought to be too permissive, too hedonistic, too self-indulgent, too irresponsible, too Godless. Those who think this is more alarmist than is justified can take scant pleasure in knowing that those who want to do away with modernism may end up with post-modernism, which they will really hate.

One of the remarkable things about the politics of the last twenty years is the degree to which President Ronald Reagan and now Newt Gingrich have been able to invoke the traditional values and images of the past while at the same time aligning themselves and their party with the high-tech future. They are very careful not to touch the delicate question of whether the consumer culture that drives much of the modern economy inevitably gives rise to the set of values that the cultural conservatives deplore. Does rational, scientific, market capitalism inevitably produce the sort of modernist, popular, nihilistic, consumer culture to which its enthusiastic supporters object? This is analogous to Seymour Martin Lipset's argument in his book, *American Exceptionalism*, that the demonstrably higher commitment of Americans to go-it-alone individu-alism also means higher levels of crime, violence, drug and alcohol abuse, and family breakdown. Indeed, go-it-alone individualism may be the problem rather than the solution.

Indeed, the cultural and political forces in our world are turning upside down. They are restructuring themselves without it being clear yet what the emerging order will be. Since the 1960s, there has been a complete inversion of the usual orientation of the contending political forces, so that American conservatism now presents itself to the public as the party of hope and of a sunny future, while American liberalism is confused and speaks in the voice of Chicken Little. Liberals once defended the downtrodden and outcast, but that is no longer cool in our self-regarding world. Liberals see problems aplenty, but conservatives have successfully convinced the public that the government is not the appropriate agency to resolve those mounting problems.

The reasons for the Culture War itself are not mysterious. First and foremost, it is a counterrevolution seeking to bridge the cultural chasm of the 1960s, the fissure that separates post-1960s America from the 1950s. The admirable core of that decade of ferment consists of the social justice movements and the anti-war movement. The former transformed the monochromatic main-stream into cultural technicolor, and the latter had the misfortune of being morally right in a way that unsettled America's view of itself as being innocent, successful and righteous. We have not yet fully integrated the results of the 1960s into our habits of thought and our daily lives.

It is significant that the active social justice issues of the second half of the twentieth century have been about race and gender, issues of cultural values, rather than about class or economic issues. Gender equity and racial equality have now been accepted by the public as American principles, a huge leap forward from the 1950s. Accordingly, it is no longer possible for a major national figure or group to appear to be racist or sexist. So, if the counterrevolution cannot be overtly intolerant, it must use flanking movements and diversionary tactics. Now, I am not saying that all of conservatism is covertly racist and sexist; and I am certainly not saying that all the changes that occurred in the 1960s were good. I don't believe either of those things, and neither should you.

I *am* saying, however, that there are reasons that "conservatism triumphant" focuses as it does on cultural issues. First, the Republican coalition is an unstable alliance of three elements: traditional business conservatives, libertarians, and cultural and religious conservatives. Their goals are not really the same. The libertarians want minimal government. While business conservatives want less government interference, they also need government to promote their interests abroad, to guarantee honest markets and fair competition at home, and to maintain stable economic conditions. The cultural right utters strong anti-government rhetoric, but they also want government to intervene and enforce their notions of personal morality. Not only do these three elements disagree about the role of government, but their economic interests are in conflict because they are drawn from different classes and different sectors of the economy. The cultural issues thus provide the political glue. It is no accident that the Culture Wars accelerated significantly after the end of the Cold War in 1989. With anti-Communism no longer available as a binding trans-economic force, cultural issues became even more important.

There is another explanation that also has some plausibility. America has traditionally had a very weak federal government. With the growth of large corporations in the late nineteenth and early twentieth centuries, progressive reformers realized that private concentrations of economic power could oppress the people as much as an autocratic government. Progressives of the twentieth century consequently turned to the federal government as the countervailing force that could protect individuals from organized economic power. That project achieved great success through the New Deal, Fair Deal, New Frontier and Great Society. Indeed, charge the conservatives, the progressive project has been too successful; it has produced the Leviathan State, complete with welfare cheats, arrogant and corrupt labor unions, wasteful government enterprises, and dependent people who are being weened away from the great American tradition of self-reliance. The Conservative project therefore is twofold: to disassemble the Leviathan State, and to roll back the cultural changes of the 1960s.

What has all of this got to do with education? Well, education at every level and of every sort, public as well as private, is part of the cultural topography. Education is thus a natural site for cultural contestation. Schools are not only critically important in our culture, but they deal with the very issues of values and history and identity that are the ostensible subject of the struggle. Even though education is local and highly decentralized, it occupies a huge amount of space in the national conversation.

It is true that the Culture Wars have abated. The NEH still lives, as does the NEA, though the Republican leadership in the House of Representatives has just promised leaders of the Christian Coalition and allied groups that it would see to it that the NEA is demolished. I do not believe they will succeed in that quest for a cultural trophy to present to the cultural and religious Right. Nevertheless, my inbred Calvinism whispers that the forces of light should not be complacent.

I worry most about the steady stream of fashionable criticism of higher education that began, perhaps, with Secretary of Education William Bennett's high profile attacks on Stanford's curriculum and the alleged intellectual corruption of the academy in general, but that continued with Allan Bloom's surprise best-seller of 1987, *The Closing of the American Mind*, which was followed by Charles Sykes' *ProfScam: Professors and the Demise of Higher Education*, Roger Kimball's *Tenured Radicals*, Dinesh D'Sousa's *Illiberal*

Education, Richard Bernstein's *Dictatorship of Virtue*, and more recently by Lynne Cheney's *Telling the Truth*.

The theme of these books is that intellectual anarchy reigns in higher education; there is no agreement about what an educated person should know. College campuses have capitulated to poststructuralism and postmodernism so that there are no fixed meanings anymore, and certainly nothing bearing the name of Truth. Every statement is taken to be a political statement, and the meaning of every text is dependent on the context of the author and the reader. The Great Western Tradition (the best that has been written and thought—as Lynne Cheney keeps reminding us that Matthew Arnold proclaimed in the 19th century) has been fatally adulterated with "politically correct" respresentives of every currently fashionable victim group. Moreover, this argument continues, objective standards and rationality have been replaced as tests of truth by other political agendas of the Left. In summary, we are being told through an orchestrated vocabulary that a "cultural elite" is undermining traditional values on which our culture depends.

I do not claim that this caricature of higher education dominates popular attitudes. Indeed, the real world appears to career along its historical rut, oblivious to the dire subversions of either the Left or the Right. Despite postmodern theory's assault on the meta-narrative of progress from scientific rationality, attended by much handwringing about the fate of the university in a world in which the possibility of knowledge has ended, the scientific and engineering worlds are booming, students and teachers converse as if they understand what is being said by the other, and post-colonial societies hanker after material goods made possible by old-fashioned modernity.

Nor do I think the critics have been successful in convincing the public that faculty are lazy and arrogant, that they pay little attention to undergraduate education, that they spend their days learning more and more about less and less, and that they then report their findings in abstruse jargon that can only be understood by half a dozen specialists around the world, but you can find those stereotypes in a lot of mainstream reportage. The stage has been set; the plotline has been established; and the university has been cast in the role of Darth Vader.

With the narrative already lying dormant in the public mind, it will require only an incident that strikes the fancy of a journalist who can use the incident to illustrate the familiar story. As Robert Hughes has observed in *Time* magazine, this semi-coordinated attack is designed "to defoliate the liberal habitat." I probably do not have to remind you where the critics think that liberal habitat is.

This does not mean, of course, that the voices from the opposite direction, accusing the university of hegemonic oppression fostered by Dead White European Males, have quieted. They are still there, though considerably muted, and their presence makes it even more likely that the press will find something to feed on.

The schools from kindergarten through high school are meanwhile engaged in a parallel drama in which the actors speak slightly different lines, but the plot is the same. Given the centrality of self-perfection as an American cultural commandment, and given the historical engagement of schools with just the sorts of issues of values, character, history and identity that are being contested in the wider society, schools cannot avoid being a battleground in the Culture Wars.

Moreover, the public has been convinced that schools are failing, though each family's actual school appears to be like the children in Lake Woebegone, above average. There is a way of looking at the history of American education since World War II that is a success story, but that is not my intent here. I am merely pointing to a mismatch among public perceptions, public expectations, and the realities of schooling. With almost a quarter of our children being raised in poverty, and with unequal and unfair distribution of educational resources, schools have an impossible task of being successful in the eyes of their critics. They are thus even more vulnerable than colleges to the destructive effects of blunderbuss reform imposed from the outside. The assassination of bilingual education in California at the hands of Proposition 227 in a statewide referendum is the most recent case on point. The seductive and destructive lure of vouchers is lurking in the shadows.

Fortunately, in America, we have never been governed by a pure theory, but by an eclectic system of thought that depends very heavily on the interaction of apparently opposed concepts and bodies of theory and values. In this way we can benefit from the complementary attributes of classical liberal and classical republican ideas, from the simultaneous pursuit of individual **liberty** AND **equality**, from the realization that we are all **products** of our culture and at the same time **authors** of our culture, from the mutually reinforcing relationships between our respect for **individualism** and our love of **community**.

One of the major tasks of education in our mixed system is to help individuals understand enough about themselves and how the world works to be able to choose their own values and fashion their own identities. Indeed, the great aim and end of all learning is to enable us to help shape our culture and our communities so as to allow all of us the power to fulfill our potential.

The "pursuit of happiness" that appears in the Declaration means the freedom to develop one's own capacities, to improve oneself, even to choose one's own identity. It is true that no one starts his life-of-choosing unencumbered by outside influences. We are all situated in time and place and race and gender and class. Unless we make an effort, our choices are shaped for us by our cultural contexts. Especially is this true of the least well-off among us. Education, however, can set us free, can give us the power not only to be who we want to be, but to imagine all the kinds of people we have the potential to become. In a culture that places so much emphasis upon self-definition and self-improvement, education occupies a critical position, one that is both privileged and vulnerable.

Our correct response to this particular cultural and political moment depends on our understanding the symbiotic relationship between **individualism** and **community**, their interdependence. We can't afford to fall into the error of binary thinking, in which individualism and community are thought to be in tension with each other. In that conception of the situation, the best we can do is to try to keep them somehow in balance because they are pictured as defining an axis of a zero sum game. If we have more individualism, we will have less community. That is simply wrong.

To be sure, America is powerfully about self-perfection, but we have always understood intuitively that the individual cannot perfect himself apart from his community. For instance, when a nationally representative sample of Americans is asked to register either positive or negative reactions to a list of words, the feelings are overwhelmingly positive at the mention of "individualism"; but the reactions are also overwhelmingly positive at the mention of "community."

In American life, then, the relationship between individualism and community is dialogic. The two terms of the relationship are in conversation with each other; they inform and modify each other; neither one means the same thing by itself as it means in conjunction with the other. In a broader and more fundamental sense, our individual identities are also determined by our relationships. We are who we are because of the communities and groups to which we belong, with which we identify, to whom we feel a sense of obligation. Without being enmeshed in a rich network of relationships, we are either isolated and alone or we are just an anonymous part of a mob.

Ask yourself the question, "Do I want to live in a society divided between the super rich and the super poor?" I hope the answer is obvious, even for those who would imagine themselves in the privileged part of that bimodal distribution. Our own lives are improved if our neighbors are well educated and prosperous. It is therefore in our interest to foster measures that help our neighbors. Our individualism depends on our community.

My own belief is that our individual fates are linked together in the quest for meaning and identity, and that ultimately we cannot be who we want to be unless others in our society have the same power. Therefore, whatever one's notion of a just society and a life worth living, education plays a critical role. Our task is to help it fulfill its promise in these trying times just ahead.

Appendix 3

QUESTIONS FOR THE RECORD BY SENATOR
KASSEBAUM FOR SHELDON HACKNEY, NOMINEE
FOR CHAIRMAN OF THE NATIONAL ENDOWMENT
FOR THE HUMANITIES

1. *Regarding the Eden Jacobowitz affair, did you think the charge of racial harassment against Mr. Jacobowitz was justified? If so, please explain why.*

I did not think the charge of racial harassment was justified. Penn's policy is very narrowly focused. It applies only in situations in which racial or ethnic slurs are used in face to face encounters and with no other intent than to inflict harm. The facts of the case do not meet these criteria.

In addition, because of the misapplication of the policy and the confusions that abound in this case, I have come to feel that even though civility is very important in an educational setting, it is a mistake to try to enforce it among members of the campus community through rules and penalties administered through a judicial system.

2. *In retrospect, do you believe you should have intervened in the university judicial process brought against Mr. Jacobowitz, or do you stand by your action not to intervene?*

As awful as the spring was, I still think it was not appropriate for me to intervene in the judicial procedure. There is no provision for the President or for any officer of the University to intervene. To have intervened would have called into question the legitimacy of the entire system that handles dozens of cases every year, denied to the complainants their right to have their complaint adjudicated by a faculty-student hearing panel, and thrown the campus into an even more divisive crisis than the one through which it actually lived. Had the system worked properly, and a hearing panel heard the case, I believe that justice would have prevailed. As it turned out, the case came to a close when the complainants withdrew their charges.

3. *In the episode involving the theft of 14,000 copies of the Daily Pennsylvanian, the University's student newspaper, in April, 1993, please explain your reaction at the time of the incident, including the complete statement issued by your office.*

I append the statements issued at the time of the incident. I believe they make clear that I recognized the seriousness of the violation and emphasized the primacy of free speech on a university campus.

4. *Please describe in detail what your administration did to identify and bring charges against those responsible for the Daily Pennsylvanian theft. Has anyone ever been charged in the theft? If so, what was the result in terms of penalties meted out?*

The Committee on Open Expression (an important faculty-student committee that monitors the Open Expression Guidelines) has ruled that the incident was a violation of the Open Expression Guidelines, thus making clear that charges would be brought. A number of students apparently involved in the incident have been identified and will face judicial procedures when they return to campus for the fall term. The one senior involved has had a "judicial hold" put on his transcript, meaning his degree, or being able to have his transcript sent to employers or graduate schools. In view of the seriousness of this case, the Vice Provost for University Life has appointed a respected senior faculty member to serve as the Special Judicial Inquiry Officer for this case.

5. *Do you believe your response to the incident was appropriate considering the seriousness of the act in the context of First Amendment rights to free expression?*

Yes, although I do wish now that in my original statement I had not used a formulation that was so easily taken out of context and misrepresented. If I could write the document again, I would undoubtedly use language that was even clearer and stronger in condemning the confiscations.

6. *Your response to the Jacobowitz affair and to the newspaper theft incident have been characterized as employing a double standard on the issue of free expression. What is your response to that charge.*

The charge is absolutely false. Throughout my career, I have defended free inquiry, free speech, and academic freedom for people from all parts of the political spectrum, left, right, and center. I have repeatedly done so when under considerable pressure to cancel appearances of controversial speakers or to discipline students or faculty who have earned the disapproval of persons or groups on campus and off. The list of speakers whose security arrangements I have personally supervised is a veritable Who's Who of controversy over the past 20 years, from William Shockley to Louis Farrakhan and all shades of opinion in between.

One incident in particular has been used to suggest that I am less than even handed. In the early 1980s, the South African Ambassador to the United States accepted an invitation to speak from a student group. The student group was then informed that University policy (which preceded my arrival at Penn) required host groups to pay all the costs of invited speakers, including security costs. Special security required for the South African Ambassador would have incurred substantial costs. The student group therefore withdrew the invitation. As soon as I heard of this situation and realized that it was based on a University policy, I changed the policy. The University isn't really open to all points of view if a host group is required to be rich enough to pay the costs involved in keeping opponents of the speaker from disrupting the event. The new policy was thus in effect when all subsequent speakers, including Louis Farrakhan, have been invited to speak on campus.

7. *The Wall Street Journal reported that at the time of a speaking engagement by artist Andres Serrano on the University of Penn campus in 1989-90, you refused to order the removal of campus sidewalk graffiti depicting anti-religious and graphic sexual symbols. Please explain what occurred.*

As with so much that the *Wall Street Journal* has reported about me, the facts are wrong in important respects, highly distorted in other respects, and the story presented in a misleading way. Early on the morning of April 13, 1993, members of Penn's groundskeeping crew arrived on campus to find, written in chalk, graffiti depicting religious and sexual graphics and offensive symbols and slogans on Locust Walk, the main pedestrian thoroughfare intersecting the Penn campus. The groundskeeping crew, on its own initiative, immediately washed off this graffiti. Later that day the students—members of a gay rights group on campus—who had originally done the graffiti writing, protested to Penn's Assistant Vice Provost for Student Life that the erasure of the graffiti violated the University's Guidelines on Open Expression. The Committee on Open Expression, following precedent, found that the graffiti was protected speech as long as the graffiti was temporary and did not permanently deface University property.

Members of the group returned the next day and renewed their graffiti writing. The issue was handled under regular University open expression policies and procedures. I was not personally involved in it. The incident did not relate to Andres Serrano's visit to Penn, which took place on December 5, 1990.

8. *Please explain your criticism of the Helms Amendment as it pertained to the work of artists, Robert Mapplethorpe and Andres Serrano.*

I did criticize the language of the Senate amendment to the NEA-NEH appropriation bill for FY90 (the Helms Amendment) because I believed that the language of the bill—which Congress wisely did not include in the final version of the appropriations legislation—was impossibly vague and overbroad. The Helms amendment to the FY90 appropriations bill would have imposed unworkable restrictions, and I believe that Congress has been wise in its judgment not to adopt it.

9. *The Wall Street Journal reported that your proposed banning ROTC from the University of Pennsylvania campus in 1990 because of the military's prohibition on gays and lesbians serving in the military. Is this true?*

As with a number of other assertions made by the *Wall Street Journal*, this is simply untrue. I am a supporter of ROTC on campus. Indeed, I am a product of the NROTC program at Vanderbilt University, and I have spoken frequently on campus about why I think it is a good program.

10. *You have been quoted in the past as stating that the impact of "political correctness" on American university campuses is "greatly exaggerated." Do you believe that "political correctness" contributes to the free exchange of ideas and tolerance of different points of view in American academia today?*

The term "political correctness" is almost hopelessly vague and imprecise. It began as a term of self-derision, and now it has taken on a life of its own as a caricature of a certain kind of liberal-left orthodoxy that is so solicitous of the interests of groups that can claim the status of have been victimized by society that the general interests of the University are of secondary importance and at times even the search for truth is threatened. Fortunately, "political correctness" does not dominate American campuses, though it is something about which faculty and academic leaders ought to worry about. I believe that I am representative of the broad mainstream of the American professoriate that sees danger lurking in any potentially intolerant orthodoxy, but that may also see some merit in the positions deemed to be politically correct. Eternal vigilance is the price of an intellectually vibrant and free campus. No single orthodoxy should ever capture a campus; the debate should remain open to any competing ideas. It is appropriate for "politically correct" ideas to be voiced on contemporary issue, but they should not be the only ideas tolerated, and they are not.

NOTES

Introduction

[1] *Washington Times*, June 26, 1993.

[2] Robert Bork's nomination to the Supreme Court by President Ronald Reagan failed in 1987 after an intense campaign by liberal organizations. Lani Guinier had been nominated by President Clinton to be the Assistant Attorney General for Civil Rights. Her nomination was withdrawn by the President when it became very controversial and before her confirmation hearing. For the full story, see Lani Guinier, *Lift Every Voice: Turning a Civil Rights Setback Into A New Vision of Social Justice* (New York: Simon and Schuster, 1998).

[3] Betty Friedan, *The Feminine Mystique* (New York: Dell Publishing Company, 1984).

[4] Robert Darnton, "All the News That Fits We Print," in *The Kiss of Lamourette: Reflections in Cultural History* (New York: W. W. Norton Company, Inc., 1990), pp. 60-93.

[5] *Ibid.*, p. 86.

Chapter 1

[1] The University interpreted that ancient obligation to mean the financial equivalent of 125 full tuition grants at any one time, and we awarded those funds on the basis of financial need. PILCOP, the Public Interest Law Center of Philadelphia, charged that Penn should be awarding 125 scholarships in each class, or 500 at any one time. The University eventually won the suit.

[2] As I write this in the fall of 1999, Harvard University has just announced that it has already raised over $2.3 billion, exceeding its goal of $2.1 for a five-year campaign due to conclude at the end of the year. Stanford held the record briefly in 1992 for raising $1.3 billion; Penn finished its campaign at $1.4 billion in 1994; Michigan matched that figure in 1997; Cornell finished its campaign in 1995 at $1.5 billion; and Yale counted $1.7 at the close of its campaign in 1997. Columbia University, riding the crest of a remarkable economy, is on its way to surpassing the extraordinary record that Harvard just established.

[3] As it turned out, for reasons that I do not now remember, I ended up talking at Convocation about something else entirely.

[4] The History Department was temporarily displaced from Dickenson Hall while it was being renovated.

[5] Neil Rudenstine (future president of Harvard) moved from Dean of Students to Dean of the College; Adele Simmons (future president of Hampshire College and of the MacArthur Foundation) joined us as Dean of Students; Alvin Kernan came from Yale to be the Dean of the Graduate School; legendary Princeton teacher and administrator Aaron Lemonick was Dean of the Faculty; Polly Bunting (former president of Radcliffe College) was the wise counselor who helped us to think carefully about a wide array of problems; Henry Bessire continued as Vice President for Development; Paul Firstenberg came from the Ford Foundation to be VP for Finance; Carl Schaefer was Treasurer; and Tony Maruca was VP for Human Resources.

[6] See Appendix I for my extended analysis of universities as the site of the culture wars, "Higher Education as a Medium of Culture," *American Behavioral Scientist* (March 1999), 987-997. Appendix treats the same phenomenon from a different angle, "Education and Democracy."

[7] http://www.goACTA.org/

[8] As I recall, this included Barbara Stevens, Linda Hyatt, Carol Farnsworth, John Gould, and Janet Hale, who had just joined Penn as Executive Vice President.

Chapter 2

[1] *New York Times*, April 15, 1988.

[2] *Almanac*, April 12, 1988.

[3] A point noted by Dan Rottenberg in his perceptive, against-the-grain op-ed pieces during this controversy. See Rottenberg, "The Journal's Insidious Portrayal of Hackney," *Philadelphia Inquirer*, July 24, 1993.

[4] Steven A. Holmes, "Survey Finds Race-Relations Gap In Armed Services, Despite Gains," *New York Times*, November 23, 1999.

[5] Gregory Pavlik, "Notes From The Laundry Room," *Daily Pennsylvanian*, February 25, 1993.

[6] Carl Bowman, *The State of Disunion*, reports the results of a survey done by the Gallup Organization for The Post-Modernity Project at the University of Virginia, directed by James Hunter. *Taking America's Pulse: The National Conference Survey on Inter-Group Relations* (March 1994), conducted by L. H. Research, study director Louis Harris.

[7] Lawrence Bobo, "The Color Line, the Dilemma, and the Dream: Race Relations in America at the Close of the Twentieth Century," and Douglas Massey, "Residential Segregation and Persistent Urban Poverty," in John Higham (ed.), *Civil Rights and Social Wrongs: Black-White Relations Since World War II* (University Park: The Pennsylvania State University Press, 1997), pp. 31-55, and 102-116.

[8] Thomas C. Grey, "Slogans, Amens, and Speech Codes," *Academic Questions* (Summer 1997), pp. 18-24.

[9] *Almanac*, July 12, 1994.

[10] Academe Today, *Chronicle of Higher Education*, (daily@chronicle.com), October 5, 1998.

[11] See, for instance, Ralph Vigoda, "Penn State Students Get Racist E-Mail," *Philadelphia Inquirer* (November 6, 1999).

[12] John Agresto, "Truth v. Liberty: A Confusion of Priorities," *Academic Questions* (Summer 1999), pp. 16-23.

Chapter 3

[1] Kors, "Thought Reform 101," *Reason Magazine* (March 2000). http://www.reasonmag.com/0003/fe.ak.thought.html

[2] Alan Kors to Sheldon Hackney, February 23, 1993. In the author's possession.

[3] Alan Kors and Harvey Silverglate, *The Shadow University: The Betrayal of Liberty on America's Campuses* (New York: The Free Press, 1998), p. 3.

[4] Alan Kors, "Kors: Penn, Hackney Mishandled 'Water Buffalo' Case," *Daily Pennsylvanian*, December 7, 1998.

[5] Kors and Silverglate, *The Shadow University*, pp. 24-25.

[6] I have chosen not to name the women complainants, nor the JIO, the JAO, or some of the other principals in the disciplinary case, in order to spare them the burden of having their names linked to a case whose meaning to the general public they had no chance to influence. Naming Kors and Jacobowitz is unavoidable, and they also chose to become public figures.

[7] Dan Rottenberg, independent journalist and frequent contributor to the op-ed page of the *Philadelphia Inquirer*, is one of the few journalists I have found who understood all the nuances of the situation, especially the "teachable moment" aspect. He did not approve of "hate speech" regulations, but he thought it was remarkable that the campus was diverse enough so that the question could come up. For him, it was something to be celebrated. See his op-ed, *Philadelphia Inquirer*, July 24, 1993.

[8] I am thinking particularly of Accuracy in Academia, the National Association of Scholars, and the American Council of Trustees and Alumni.

[9] Alan Charles Kors to Alvin V. Shoemaker, undated. Shoemaker to Kors, August 4, 1993. Xerox copies in the author's possession.

[10] For more on this remarkable woman, see her oral autobiography, edited by Hollinger F. Barnard, *Outside the Magic Circle* (Tuscaloosa: University of Alabama Press, 1985).

[11] Kors and Silverglate, *Shadow University*, p. 31.

[12] http://www.whitehouse.gov/wh/eop/first_lady/other/1993-05-17; or see *Almanac* May 18, 1993 for excerpts.

[13] *St. Petersburg Times*, May 19,1993.

[14] Transcript of the CNN program obtained from Nexis. See also Michael Kinsley, "Right Wing P.C. is Still P.C., *Time* (August 9, 1993), p. 66.

[15] May 26, 1993.

[16] *Newsday*, May 31, 1993.

[17] *Daily Pennsylvanian*, April 5, 1994.

[18] *Almanac*, September 14, 1993.

Chapter 4

[1] *Wall Street Journal*, June 25, 1993.
[2] *Washington Times*, May 25, 1993.
[3] *Wall Street Journal*, June 25, 1993.
[4] *Washington Post*, June 25, 1993.

Chapter 5

[1] Kay Graham, another Vineyard friend, arranged for me to have a lunch and discussion with the editorial board of the *Post* later in my Washington experience, and the *Post* was importantly supportive of the NEH.

Chapter 6

[1] The *Wall Street Journal* ran five editorials supporting Carol Iannon, and the *Washington Post* contributed thirteen! See *Lingua Franca*, October 1991.

Chapter 7

[1] Amy Schwartz, "What Hackney Actually Said," *Washington Post*, July 1, 1993.
[2] See Appendix III.
[3] See Appendix III.
[4] *Washington Post*, August 4, 1993.
[5] *Chronicle of Higher Education*, August 11, 1993.

Appendix 1

[1] By postmodern, I mean that collection of theories and intellectual stances that call into question scientific rationalism's claim to provide humankind with access to absolute knowledge and universal truths. It includes poststructuralism, critical theory, and deconstruction. A particularly influential statement of postmodernism proper is, Jean Francois Lyotard, *The Postmodern Condition: A Report on Knowledge* (Mineapolis: University of Minnesota Press, 1984), Translated from the original French edition of 1979 by Geoff Bennington and Brian Massumi; Foreward by Frederick Jameson. The most perceptive and most sensible discussion of postmodernism and associated concepts as they affect the writing of History is Joyce Appleby, Lynn Hunt, and Margaret Jacob, *Telling The Truth About History* (New York: W.W. Norton and Company, 1994).
[2] The South lagged these rates among the white population and deliberately repressed literacy among slaves.
[3] Clark Kerr, *The Uses of the University* (New York: Harper Torchbooks, 1966), p. 114. Originally published in 1964 by the Harvard University Press.
[4] I am using "culture" here and throughout in its Anthropological sense, as opposed to its aesthetic sense as referring to self-conscious expressions of truth and beauty in the arts and humanities. Though no definition has universal

assent, I mean by "culture" the conventional ways of believing and behaving, that complex of values and meanings that is shared among a group of people, who indeed are defined as belonging to a common category by their sharing of those beliefs and behaviors.

[5] Betty Friedan, *The Feminine Mystique* (New York: Dell Publishing Company, 1984).

[6] Allan Bloom, *The Closing of the American Mind: How Higher Education Has Failed Democracy and Impoverished the Souls of Today's Students* (New York: Simon & Schuster, 1987). Roger Kimball, *Tenured Radicals: How Politics Has Corrupted Our Higher Education* (New York: Harper and Row, Publishers, 1990). Dinesh D'Souza, *Illiberal Education: The Politics of Race and Sex on Campus* (New York: Free Press, 1991). Richard Bernstein, *Dictatorship of Virtue: How the Battle of Multiculturalism is Reshaping Our Schools, Our Country, Our Lives* (New York: Alfred A. Knopf, 1994). Lynne Cheney, *Telling the Truth: Why Our Culture and Our Country Have Stopped Making Sense and What We Can Do About It* (New York: Simon & Schuster, 1995). Alan Kors and Harvey A. Silverglate, *The Shadow Univesity: The Betrayal of Liberty on America's Campuses* (New York: Free Press, 1998).

[7] The flavor of this critique can be sampled in Walter Berns, "The Assault on the Universities: Then and Now," in Stephen Macedo (ed.) *Reasessing the Sixties: Debating the Political and Cultural Legacy* (New York: W. W. Norton & Company, 1997), pp. 157-183.

[8] Robert Hughes, "Pulling the Fuse on Culture," *Time Magazine* (August 7, 1995), cover story.

[9] See the classic history, Laurence R. Veysey, *The Emergence of the American University* (Chicago: The University of Chicago Press, 1965), especially Chapter 4.

[10] For a combative, point-by-point refutation of Allan Bloom's argument, see Lawrence W. Levine, *The Opening of the American Mind: Canons, Culture, and History* (Boston: Beacon Press, 1996). For a gentler tracing of the content of the curriculum from the eighteenth century on, see W. B. Carnochan, *The Battleground of the Curriculum: Liberal Education and American Experience* (Stanford: Stanford University Press, 1993). The general point to be derived from these two histories is that the curriculum has always been a contentious matter about which faculties have had trouble agreeing, that it has evolved in response to various forces intrnal and exernal, and that the Great Books and Western Civilization approaches, much beloved of cultural critics as *the tradition*, are only about seventy-five years old.

[11] David Lodge, *Small World: An Academic Romance* (New York: Warner Books, 1984). p. 29.

[12] Nigel Blake argues that the two threats to the university at the moment are (1) becoming a Tower of Babel, and (2) becoming merely a think tank for society's current problems. "Truth, Identity and Community in the University," in Ronald Barnett and Anne Griffin (eds.), *The End of Knowledge* (London: Cassell, 1997), pp. 151-164.

Index

About the Author

Sheldon Hackney is currently Professor of History at the University of Pennsylvania. Previously, he served four years as Chairman of the National Endowment for the Humanities (1993-97); from 1981 to 1993 he was President of the University of Pennsylvania; from 1975 to 1981 he was President of Tulane University. He was on the history faculty at Princeton University from 1965 to 1975, serving as Provost of the University the final three of those years.

Professor Hackney's *Populism to Progressivism* in Alabama (Princeton Press, 1969; reissue forthcoming in 2003 from NewSouth Books) was awarded the Beveridge Prize by the American Historical Association as the best book in American History that year, and the Sydnor Prize by the Southern Historical Association as the best book in Southern history in that two year period. In addition, he has edited several collections of essays and articles, and has published widely in newspapers and journals on history, higher education, and American culture. Professor Hackney received the Lindback Teaching Award from Penn in 2001.

Professor Hackney has served on numerous Boards, including the American Council on Education, the Carnegie Foundation for the Advancement of Teaching, the Educational Testing Service, the Rosenbach Museum andLibrary, the National Constitution Center, and the American Forum for Global Education.

Dr. Hackney received his undergraduate degree from Vanderbilt University and his M.A. and Ph.D. degrees from Yale. He lives in Philadelphia with his wife, Lucy Durr Hackney, a lawyer and children's advocate. They have three children and eight grandchildren.

The Politics of Presidential
Appointment

DATE DUE			